Hiring&Firing

What Every Manager Needs to Know

Revised Edition

Hiring&Firing

What Every Manager Needs to Know

by Marlene Caroselli, Ed.D.

SkillPath Publications
Mission, KS

Editor
Kelly Scanlon

Contributing Editor
Laura J. Wyeth, M.S. Ed.

Page Layout
Francine Bizal

Cover Design
Rod Hankins

Library of Congress Catalog Card Number: 95-71719
ISBN: 1-878542-35-4

10   9   8   7   6   5   4   3   2   96   97   98   99   00

Printed in the United States of America

Contents

Table of Worksheets

Part One: The Hiring Process

Part Two: The Firing Process

Introduction

Just as a good debater anticipates the position of his or her opponent, so, too, does a good interviewer understand what a good interviewee is likely to do and vice versa. Just as a football team with a fierce desire to win will study the taped performance of its strongest competitor, so will a supervisor be prepared for the questions or reactions of the person who has to be fired. Just as a quality-driven organization will benchmark to learn what the best companies in the field do, so will the successful supervisor learn as much as possible about the processes of hiring and firing, considering the processes from both viewpoints: interviewer/interviewee during the hiring process and supervisor/ employee during the firing process.

If you have taken the time to purchase and read this book, you must be interested in making the processes professional. A win-win situation is the aim of all hiring situations. But is it possible, you are probably wondering, to make firing a win-win situation? Without a doubt. But both processes require time, effort, and practice on your part. Reading this book is the first step toward becoming a supervisor who can hire and fire, if need be, with both confidence and a clear conscience.

Whether you are hiring or firing, the process involves three stages: things to be done *before, during,* and *after* the interview or meeting with the person you will hire or fire. And although you, as a supervisor, are currently in a position to hold these interviews or meetings, the day may come when you yourself may be in the opposite position. Should you ever have the exciting opportunity to work for a new company, you will want to turn to this book again and read about the hiring and firing processes from a different perspective.

This book offers an active, "hands-on" approach to hiring and firing. As you read through the book, you will be asked to evaluate your own hiring and firing situations and to complete exercises designed to reinforce the concepts presented in the book.

To guide you through the book, we have built in several recurring features, including:

- Quick tips.

- Figures.

- Summary grids.

- Worksheets.

- Success strategies.

Quick tips. Several lists of highlighted items appear throughout the chapters. These lists are intended to function as "tips" that highlight the actions, steps, or processes necessary for achieving "win-win" hiring and firing situations.

Figures. The figures are designed to visually illustrate concepts that have been presented in the text.

Summary grids. The concepts presented in each section, or part, of the book, are summarized in a grid at the end of Part 1 and Part 2. Review these summary grids to quickly recall the information discussed in each section.

Worksheets. The worksheets are intended as exercises you can use to enhance your understanding of the concepts presented in the book. The rationale behind these worksheets is to get you to focus now on ways to improve your hiring and firing skills. Answers to the worksheets are provided in Appendix C.

Success strategies. Throughout the book, business leaders share their hiring and firing strategies with you.

Appendix A contains forms designed to organize the steps involved in the hiring process. Appendix B contains forms for focusing the procedures and documentation required in a firing situation.

By the time you have completed this book, you should be better equipped to answer the following questions:

- How do I create an applicant pool?

- What kinds of questions are effective in an interview?

- What kinds of questions and actions might invite a lawsuit?

- What can I do to ensure that the interview itself proceeds smoothly?

- How do I document the information I obtain during the employment interview?

- What steps do I take once I have selected a person to fill the position?
- What is downsizing, as opposed to individual firings?
- What type of documentation is necessary during disciplinary meetings?
- How do I get at the source of an employee's problem?
- What steps should I follow during an actual termination meeting?
- How do I deal with other employees who are uneasy about the termination?

Before you begin, take a few minutes to complete Worksheet 1. It will help you focus on your past hiring and firing encounters and provide you with a springboard for comparing your past actions with the suggestions discussed in this book.

> **"A great deal may be done by severity, more by love, but most by clear discernment and impartial justice."**
>
> —*Jonathan Peter Eckerman*

✍ Worksheet 1
Past Hiring and Firing Experiences

1. Describe how you felt the last time you had to hire or fire
   someone. (If you have never had to do either, describe how
   you felt the last time you were hired or fired.)

   _____

   _____

   _____

   _____

   _____

2. What preparations did you make before the employment
   interview or the termination meeting?

   _____

   _____

   _____

   _____

   _____

3. What actions did you take after the employment interview or
   the termination meeting?

   _____

   _____

   _____

   _____

   _____

4. What do you feel was the most successful aspect of that hiring
   or firing experience?

   _____

   _____

   _____

   _____

   _____

   _____

1

The Hiring Process

> **"If workers are carefully selected, the problems of discipline will be negligible."**

Johnson & Johnson Company
The Employee Relations Manual, *1932*

> **"Hiring and training are costly— but it is infinitely more costly to have a marginal or barely average man on the company rolls for 30 years."**

Gordon W. Wheeling
Personnel Manager,
Beckman & Whitley
Leadership in the Office,
ANACOM, 1963

Introduction

Human Resources. More important than natural resources, physical resources, financial resources. It is human resources that decide any organization's ultimate fate. Finding and keeping the right people for the right positions requires both knowledge and skills. The interviewer needs knowledge of the interview process and knowledge of the laws that protect applicants. The interviewer also needs skills for listening, assessing, and aligning the best candidate to the job best-suited for that candidate's talents.

If you find yourself in the serious but rewarding position of interviewing job seekers for an opening in your organization, you need to obtain the best possible guidance before scheduling your first interview. The information that follows offers you that guidance. Read the book carefully, answer the questions, consult with colleagues, and make certain you know what you are looking for. Then begin the interview process.

Keep an open mind. If a candidate appears to be underqualified but has a burning desire to work in your company, that person may, in fact, be the right person. Too, a candidate may seem overqualified but eager to work for you. Overqualified people may leave in time, but if they are rewarded for their efforts, they will often stay with a company longer than the average employee does.

If your firm utilizes psychological tests, recognize that there are some disadvantages to the results they yield. The tests may restrict your work force to a particular type of person and, thus, cut off the innovative applicant whose divergent thinking is exactly what is needed to solve some of your company's problems. Don't automatically assume that applicants who were fired from their previous positions are not right for your company. (If Chrysler had taken that point of view, the company would never have hired Lee Iacocca.)

Tests must always be job-related. Sometimes, even if a test is job-related, it may have an "adverse impact" on minorities and so may be viewed as unlawful. For example, a general test of verbal skills assessing mastery of the English language might disqualify candidates with a bilingual background. If the test is used as a basis for hiring, it can be viewed as excluding certain minorities. And if English cannot be proven to be a necessary job requirement, the test could be unlawful. Federal rules stipulate that the pass rate for minorities (including women) must be 8 percent or more of the pass rate of white men. If it is less, the testing procedure can have an "adverse impact."

Don't yield to the pressure of time. If you are not completely satisfied with the applicants you have seen, consider hiring a temporary employee to fill the job while you continue the search for the ideal candidate. (Temporary employees often prove themselves capable of holding the job permanently, by the way.) Hiring decisions should not be hasty decisions. Particularly for management positions, you should continue interviewing until you believe you have found a well-qualified candidate eager to work for your firm. Then, have the applicant start as soon as possible. Long delays between the hiring decision and the first day of work increase the likelihood that another company may make a better offer to the candidate.

The results of poor interview decisions are costly! The United States Department of Labor estimates the cost at one-third the annual salary of the newly hired person. (Some estimates place that figure as high as 50 percent of the employee's salary.) If you take the time to structure the interview professionally, you increase the chances for win-win results. Ideally, both interviewer and interviewee will leave the meeting feeling that time was well-spent and that a valuable contact was made.

Success Strategies From...

W.R. Ernisse, Vice President, Customer and Marketing Education, Xerox Corporation

On Hiring: "Too often, most of the interview time is spent with the manager describing the open job versus finding out about the applicants."

To maximize the time available during the interview, Ernisse suggests these ideas:

1. Send a position questionnaire, the position's mission statement, and a departmental organization chart to the candidate as pre-reading.

2. Develop a list of specific job requirements and an interview list of questions for all candidates and stick to that list. Emphasize questions probing the candidate's past performance in areas of related skills or situations.

3. Always make the candidate comfortable and at ease.

4. Check out references.

5. Ask the manager immediately above the hiring manager to also interview the top two candidates.

On Firing: "If termination is due to ethics, address the situation immediately in a closed conference room or office. Don't hesitate or beat around the bush. State your decision to terminate, the reason, and walk the employee out of the building. Don't apologize or get into a debate. Get all badges, keys, and so forth from the employee.

"If termination is due to performance, your actions should come as no surprise to the employee if you have followed the formal corrective processes."

1

Decide how you will find the
person to fill the position.

2

Determine the qualities and skills you
wish the candidate to have; then
revise, update, or create a
job description identifying the
essential functions of the job.

3

Prepare a list of questions that
you will ask of each candidate.

4

Take notes and prepare a form to use
in assessing applicants.

5

Choose an interview style.

6

Develop a definite plan for
conducting an interview.

1

Before the Employment Interview

As with most things in life, success comes to those who have prepared for it. The interviewing process, if it is to yield optimal results, must be carefully thought out. Here are some of the things to be done before you shake the hand of that first job applicant who walks through your door.

■ **Decide how you will find the person to fill the position.**

Finding the ideal applicant for a particular job opening is a combination of good planning, good communicating, and just plain good luck. As you begin to think about filling a position that has become available or one that has been newly created, you must decide how you will find the candidates, including where and how to advertise the position and who will be involved in the hiring process:

- Will you select from within or search outside the company?

- Will you advertise in the newspaper? If so, will you use blind ads? What will the ads say?

- Will you turn the hiring decision over to the personnel department? To some other person? Will your secretary screen the initial applicants? Will you use an employment agency?

- Is there a job description for this job? If so, does the description document the essential functions of the job? Does the description need to be revised or updated?

There are advantages and disadvantages to each of the approaches available for creating a pool of applicants. Only you can decide which approach will work best for your particular hiring situation.

For example, if you *select from within the company*, you will no doubt find someone who is familiar with the corporate mission, the established procedures, the personnel and, above all else, the firm's distinct method of producing its product or delivering its service. Sometimes, however, these internal promotions create dissension among the ranks. Employees selected above their peers often find it difficult to supervise those very peers. Of course, these considerations do not apply to entry-level positions.

Companies that fill positions from within advertise their openings in a variety of ways. According to Don Ford, human resource development consultant, companies will post job announcements on a bulletin board or through electronic mail for a specified period of time before interviews begin. In this way, companies can avoid charges of favoritism and can prevent individuals with "inside knowledge" from having an unfair advantage over others interested in the position.

Management development specialist Richard Best of Lockheed Aircraft Services Co. points out that some companies post salaried positions by way of weekly fliers. Interested individuals submit their resumés through the human resources department. Resumés of qualified candidates are sent for review to the hiring manager, who then sets up interviews with appropriate applicants.

Best notes that hourly workers who desire to upgrade their classification can contact employee relations. These employees provide evidence of their increased knowledge and skills. Then, when openings become available, the employee relations department contacts the hourly workers suited for those openings and arranges interviews.

Many organizations like to *search outside the company*, not only to bring "fresh blood" into the company but also to develop a wide base of respondents to their classified ads. Some companies that hire from outside the company view the newspaper as an inexpensive means of seeking applicants. The disadvantage to running an ad is that many unqualified candidates will respond to the limited specifications listed in the advertisement. Someone needs to screen the respondents prior to setting up interviews. Otherwise, much valuable time will be wasted: yours as well as the applicant's!

Blind ads do not identify the company that is seeking to fill a job. Instead, prospects are asked to send resumés to a post office box. Companies sometimes use blind ads so that the person who is about to be dismissed does not realize replacements are already being lined up for the job. Blind ads are also used when companies expect a heavy response to the ad and do not want to be inundated with telephone inquiries about the position.

If you *turn the hiring decision over to the personnel department*, you will need to ensure that the job description for the position is accurate, specific, and up-to-date. Care should be taken to include only those functions and abilities that are actually job related. Close communication between you and the personnel department is necessary so that the department truly interviews for the kind of employee you are seeking. Are there others within the organization who may be able to carry out the preliminary seek-and-find responsibilities?

You may wish to consider an *informal "networking" approach* for finding the new employee. This approach works especially well if there is no urgency involved in replacing the current employee. In fact, you may even wish to enlist that employee's help in finding a replacement! For example, an employee who is planning to retire sometime during the year but who is not rigid about the exact month or week may be willing to inquire among friends or colleagues for someone who would be ideal for the position.

Quick Tips. . .

Creating An Applicant Pool

There are two ways to create a pool of applicants: by advertising inside the company or outside the company. Consider the advertising possibilities for each way.

Inside the Company	*Outside the Company*
➤ bulletin board announcements	➤ newspapers, including blind ads
➤ electronic mail	➤ employment agencies
➤ weekly flyers	➤ networking

Sharon Renda, a certified personnel consultant who is CEO and owner of Renda Personnel Consultants, Inc., of Rochester, New York, explains how companies ordinarily use the services of an *employment agency*. They can operate on the basis of a contingency fee, which means the company pays the fee only if someone is hired as a direct result of the agency's efforts. The company, however, is free to use other services in its search for candidates. The agency is paid only if one of its referrals is hired.

By comparison, in a search assignment, the company pays a retained fee up front and gives the agency full rein to locate the individual (usually for upper-echelon positions). Typically, with such an arrangement, the company will pay one-third the fee when the search begins, another one-third after the candidates have been narrowed down to two or three, and the final third when the interviews are complete and the candidate has been hired.

Renda stresses the importance of making candidates aware of what the company's mission is. Hiring decisions are too important and too expensive to be conducted without sharing information completely. Candidates must be apprised of the culture and nature of the company, its aims and expectations. Otherwise, subsequent dissatisfaction may set in, and the chosen candidate may become disillusioned about the job for which he or she was chosen.

Renda Personnel Consultants, Inc., keeps a pool of applicants on file and when requests come in, the company tries to match the requirements of the position with the skills of the applicants. The company also advertises if the files do not have a person well-suited to a particular job. On occasion, the firm will use a person it has already hired to suggest other possible sources for a particular job.

When requested, Renda will conduct tests for a company. The firm administers personality profiles and technical tests in addition to their own aptitude tests.

■ **Determine the qualities and skills you wish the candidate to have; then revise, update, or create a job description identifying the essential functions of the job.**

Your next consideration as you prepare for the interview is to determine the qualities and skills you feel are critical for candidates to possess. Identifying these skills requires you to break the job into its component tasks and then to isolate the competencies needed for those tasks.

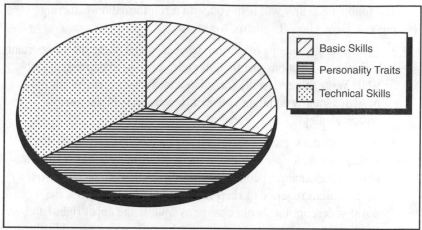

Fig. 1.   Before you design your evaluation form, decide which basic, technical, and personality skills are most relevant to the job.

The job description will determine the essential (vs. marginal) functions of the job. The essential functions must be able to be performed successfully with or without a reasonable accommodation, by a qualified individual.

Apart from the job description—which primarily lists tasks or duties for which the person will be responsible—what personality traits do you feel are important for this job? Are leadership skills or teambuilding skills needed? Do you need someone who is creative, or organized, or outgoing? Should the candidate possess good communication skills?

Consider what the jobholder should be able to do in order to perform the job well. Decide which skills and qualities and the kinds of knowledge that will lead to maximum job performance. Then decide which specific questions will reveal whether the applicant has the requisite qualifications. Also, make it your business to find out comparable salaries for the kind of job you are advertising.

You may find it useful to speak to the employee who currently holds the position to be filled in order to learn how that person would specify the requirements of the job. Conducting such an exit interview will also provide you with a fuller understanding of exactly what the job entails. You can use this information during the interview to give the applicant a more exact idea of what skills and traits are needed to do the job well.

The following matrix will help you with this information-gathering process. Here's how the matrix works:

- From your knowledge of the job, what are some of the most important activities or functions that the jobholder must do to perform the job well? Write those valuable (or value-added) tasks in the upper left-hand quadrant. You might consider these aspects of the job as critical elements.

- Next, consider some of the tasks listed on the job description that perhaps are no longer essential to performing the job well. Corporate philosophies change; people change; jobs change. In response to the modifications required to keep abreast of all these changes, the position description should change as well. In the upper right-hand quadrant, list some aspects of the job that truly no longer add value to the processes in which this particular employee engages.

- Again, from your knowledge of how the job should be performed, what are some things that you've known jobholders to do that do not need to be done. Think carefully about this one. You are concerned here with tasks the employee added to the job description, but do not add value. For example, if the job is a secretarial position, and you once had a secretary who both alphabetized and prioritized your incoming calls on two separate lists, you would note in the bottom right-hand quadrant that such excessive recordkeeping is not needed. Use the past to refine the future. Being aware of such redundant efforts will make the new jobholder more efficient.

- In the last quadrant, on the bottom left-hand side, record the comments of individuals who do or have done the job in question. These employees have probably found some shortcuts or ways to optimize their efforts, which are not officially part of the job description. Because such details will help you know the demands of the job more thoroughly, your presentation of the position to the job applicant will certainly be more accurate and more realistic.

JOB MATRIX

Employer-Defined Tasks That Add Value	Employer-Defined Tasks That Do Not Add Value
Employee-Included Tasks That Add Value	Employee-Included Tasks That Do Not Add Value

Fig. 2. Before filling any position, take time to analyze it. Talk to the current or former holder of that job to identify the officially sanctioned job requirements — those on the job description. Does the current jobholder feel that any of those requirements add little or no value to the job and, therefore, could be eliminated? Also consider the tasks that are not part of the actual job description but which are nonetheless being performed by the current jobholder. Analyzing this information will allow you to refine the job description and present an accurate picture of the job to the new applicant.

Quick Tips . . .

50 Vital Verbs

As you review resumés prior to the employment interview, search each resumé for the following verbs that indicate real accomplishment. Highlight these verbs in yellow on the resumé, and then during the interview, ask the candidate to elaborate, to explain precisely what he or she did to "implement," "modernize," and so forth.

1. initiated	26. developed
2. organized	27. engineered
3. triggered	28. established
4. launched	29. implemented
5. sparked	30. installed
6. originated	31. converted
7. instituted	32. led
8. created	33. secured
9. introduced	34. controlled
10. cut	35. procured
11. eliminated	36. discovered
12. saved	37. researched
13. prevented	38. disseminated
14. reduced	39. negotiated
15. optimized	40. prioritized
16. increased	41. coordinated
17. doubled	42. directed
18. expanded	43. modernized
19. investigated	44. improved
20. trained	45. systematized
21. analyzed	46. initiated
22. forecasted	47. designed
23. verified	48. promoted
24. arranged	49. interfaced with
25. set up	50. generated

■ Prepare a list of questions that you will ask of each candidate.

General Questions. Skilled interviewers always have specific questions that will elicit from candidates the most crucial information about their skills and abilities. The same questions should be asked of all candidates so an objective accounting can be made of their responses. And there should be a definite flow or sequence to the time spent between interviewer and interviewee.

Your first question, something such as "Tell me about yourself," should focus on putting the applicant at ease and at starting a dialogue between you and the applicant. Make sure that the questions you ask adhere to internal company policies. You must also ensure that your questions do not violate Title VII of the Civil Rights Act or Title I of the Americans with Disabilities Act. If you have doubts about which questions you can or cannot ask, check with legal counsel or do some further reading on the subject.

Choose from the questions on pages 21 to 23 the ones you feel will yield the most salient information for a given position.

"Stress" Questions. In addition to the general questions you ask each candidate, some interviewers like to pose questions that catch the candidate by surprise.

Do not ask these questions to make applicants uneasy or uncomfortable. The interviewing philosophy that virtually has the interviewer set a fire and then sit back to watch how well the applicant can handle an emergency often reveals little about how well the applicant can perform the job.

However, do ask the candidate tough, challenging questions, for they often reveal a candidate's ability to think spontaneously, to solve problems, to articulate ideas, to organize thoughts, to handle pressure, and so forth. The value of these questions is that they are not anticipated and, therefore, candidates will not have stock answers ready.

Try answering a few yourself—without pausing very long to formulate an answer. (Remember, your candidates will be expected to respond extemporaneously.) The extent of your difficulty in answering will give you some idea of how much allowance to make for candidates' difficulty. You may also wish to compare your answers with the answers colleagues give—again, in an effort to assess what constitutes a good answer from a candidate.

One last note of caution: If you do use these questions, use them near the end of the interview so that the applicant's responses do not influence you too much one way or the other. The questions are difficult but revealing. However, they should not count for more than 10 percent of the overall points in your interview rating system.

1. What was your last original thought?

2. What is your business philosophy?

3. Explain a concept to me.

4. Tell me about myself. (This question reveals a great deal about the candidate's ability to assess character, to listen, and to express ideas. It also reveals to some extent the candidate's ability to be diplomatic and intuitive.)

5. What constitutes leadership?

6. If you were president of this company, what is one new plan/policy/product you would initiate?

> **66** We hired the wrong people...
> because we were in such a hurry
> to fill those positions. **99**
>
> *Lynn Tendler Bignell*
> *Founder, Gilbert Tweed Associates*
> Inc. Magazine, *November 1987*

Quick Tips . . .

General Interview Questions

1. Tell me about yourself.
2. Why should we hire you?
3. Why are you giving up your current job?
4. What did you like best about your last job?
5. Why did you choose your particular field?
6. What qualifications do you have that make you successful in this field?
7. What is your experience?
8. Why are you interested in this job?
9. What is it that you want to do?
10. What do you know about this company?
11. What is more important to you: the salary or the job itself?
12. Do you prefer working alone or with others?
13. If you could have made improvements in your last job, what would they have been?
14. What has been the most interesting job or project so far in your career?
15. What did you major in? Why? Do you regret selecting that major?
16. What kind of people annoy you most? (Note: The applicant is probably the opposite of the type of person given as a response.)
17. Describe the best person who ever worked for you or with you.
18. What are the disadvantages associated with your chosen field?
19. What do you think determines a person's progress in a firm?
20. How would you like our company to assist you if you join us?
21. Describe some of the emergencies that forced you to rearrange your time in some of your previous jobs.
22. What is your greatest strength? Worst deficiency?
23. Describe the most significant report or presentation you have had to prepare.

24. Tell me about a time when you had to make a decision quickly.
25. How much would you like to be earning in five years?
26. How did you get along with your former boss?
27. Do you know of any reason you could not perform the job as I have described it to you?
28. Do you think you would be underemployed if you accepted this position?
29. What are your goals—both short-term and long-term?
30. What are your hobbies or pastimes?
31. Can you take instructions without being upset?
32. What have you learned from previous jobs?
33. Are you willing to relocate for the company?
34. What books or magazines do you read?
35. What do you think are the most serious problems facing business today?
36. How would you define leadership? Success?
37. What is your philosophy of business?
38. What can a department do to build teamwork?
39. What was the most creative work project you ever completed?
40. What are you best known for?
41. From whom have you learned the most?
42. What qualities, in your opinion, does an outstanding supervisor possess?
43. Do you manage your time well? Explain.
44. What are your views on quality?
45. Describe your "dream" job.
46. What problem-solution situation are you most proud of?
47. Describe a time when you were able to have a positive influence on others.
48. How flexible are you?
49. If you could have any position in this company, which would it be?
50. What motivates you?
51. How intuitive are you?
52. How do you handle conflicts?

53. Tell me about a time when you conformed to a policy you disagreed with.

54. What sort of person would you least like to work with? (Note: Again, the candidate is probably the opposite of the kind of person given as a response.)

55. Are you working toward a degree?

56. Describe a situation that required you to use fact-finding skills.

57. What can be done about employees entering the work force without proper skills?

58. How do you cope with the inevitable stresses and pressures of the job?

59. If you were me, would you hire you? Why?

60. Have you ever thought about starting your own company?

61. Tell me about a work situation that required excellent communication skills.

62. What sort of person do you enjoy working for?

63. What ways have you discovered to improve your productivity?

64. What skills or traits do you feel a successful manager should have?

65. What was the last truly innovative suggestion you made for your firm?

66. What American businessperson do you most admire and why?

67. Have you ever taken a public-speaking course?

68. Do you train others well? Please give me an example of your effectiveness.

69. How well/often do you communicate with the person who receives the output of your work?

70. What is your boss's title and what are your boss's functions?

71. How well do you think on your feet?

72. Please describe for me a typical day on your current job.

73. What accomplishment are you most proud of? (Note: A candidate who mentions other people or uses the pronoun "we" usually works well on a team.)

74. What has been your most important work-related idea?

75. What kind of references will your previous employer give you?

✍ Worksheet 2
Critical Employment Questions

Which five questions are most significant for the next employment interview you have to conduct? Write each question here, along with what you consider the ideal answer. When you are conducting the interview, compare the applicants' answers to the responses you have written on this page.

1. Question: _____

   _____

   An exemplary answer would be: _____

   _____

   _____

2. Question: _____

   _____

   An exemplary answer would be: _____

   _____

   _____

3. Question: _____

   _____

   An exemplary answer would be: _____

   _____

   _____

4. Question: _____

   _____

   An exemplary answer would be: _____

   _____

   _____

5. Question: _____

   _____

   An exemplary answer would be: _____

   _____

   _____

   _____

■ Take notes and prepare a form to use in assessing applicants.

Research shows that shortly after hearing something, we forget most of it. Our retention rate a day later is only about 25 percent. For this reason, it is imperative that you take notes while you conduct your interviews. Taking notes also benefits the applicant, for with notes you will clearly be able to differentiate one applicant from the other.

Tell the applicant that you will be taking notes throughout the interview. Use an interview form to assess the candidates and a blank sheet of paper to record other thoughts you may have. Follow the note-taking tips listed below.

Quick Tips...

Note-Taking Tips

➤ Use your own special form of shorthand.

➤ Use a clipboard so the applicant can't see what you are writing.

➤ Don't stop writing if you are surprised by something the applicant says.

➤ Do stop writing if the applicant's statements seem to demand your full attention.

The interview form you use to assess an applicant's skills should include the criteria that are most useful to you. The form does not need to be complicated, but it should cover salient points and should have room for your own notes. Fill out one form for each applicant. Figures 3 and 4 provide examples of two different kinds of interview forms. For the purpose of the examples, the forms list criteria related to a secretarial position. However, a blank copy of each of the forms is included in Appendix A. Copy them for use in interviewing, or use them as a starting point for creating a customized form suited to your particular interview style.

	INTERVIEW FORM		

Job _____ Applicant _____ Date _____

Criteria/ Critical Skills	Job Tasks	Question	Comments
1. Word processing	Extensive reports	What are your word processing skills?	
2. Accuracy	Critical info; used widely in company	Would you be willing to take a typing test?	
		How is accuracy measured in your current position?	
3. Interpersonal skills	Must relate to engineers/upper management, etc.	How do others usually describe you?	
		How do you describe yourself as a worker? What would you do if you suspected information on a report you had to type was inaccurate?	
4.			
5.			
6.			
7.			
8.			

Fig. 3.   Interview form relating critical skills associated with the job to the specific tasks that must be performed. Interview questions are based on the relationship of the skills to the job task.

Admittedly, the interview form in Figure 3 will take some time to prepare as it requires you to list all the critical skills or criteria associated with the job and to relate them to the specific tasks to be accomplished. Then you must formulate questions that will elicit information regarding the applicant's possession of those specific skills.

If you are reluctant to invest this kind of time, consider these advantages to such thoroughness:

- The form can be used any time you need to interview someone for the position.

- The form can probably be used by anyone else in your company who needs to hire for the same position.

- The form will help ensure that you find the right person for the job. Think about the time, money, and effort that are wasted when the wrong person has been selected.

The interview form in Figure 4 lists the most important skills for the job and requires you to assign a number between 1 and 10 to indicate the importance of each skill to the job. The applicant is then evaluated, again on a scale of 1 to 10, to determine competence for that particular skill. The next step is to multiply these two numbers for each skill to yield the Skills Score. Finally, the Skills Scores are tallied to yield the candidate's Total Score, which is then compared to the Total Scores for all other candidates.

■ Choose an interview style.

You can use various interview styles. Choose the one that you are most comfortable with and that will yield the results you need. Some interviewers prefer the *chatty* approach. To put the applicant at ease, they like to engage in informal discussions—about the weather or world events or the likelihood of a sports team winning the national championship. The problem with this approach is that time is often wasted discussing topics unrelated to the job.

Other interviewers use a *scripted* technique: they write down all their questions in advance and allocate approximate times for conducting each portion of the interview. This technique, on the opposite end of the interviewing continuum as the chatty approach, is efficient, but an interviewer who is not willing to deviate from the script may miss valuable information and insights.

INTERVIEW FORM

Job _____ Applicant _____ Date _____

Criteria/ Critical Skills	Importance	X	Applicant's Score	=	Skills Score
1. Word Processing Skills	10	X	9	=	90
2. Accuracy	10	X	9	=	90
3. Interpersonal Skills	10	X	9	=	90
4. _____	____	—	—	—	—
5. _____	____	—	—	—	—
6. _____	____	—	—	—	—
7. _____	____	—	—	—	—
8. _____	____	—	—	—	—

Total Score for Candidate   =   ____

Comments: _____

_____

_____

_____

Fig. 4.   Interview form utilizing a 10-point rating system to assess
candidates' possession of critical skills.

For higher level positions, some employers select *hidden-agenda* questions or situations to gain a perspective on the verbal and physical responses they feel are significant to the position. One company, for example, holds interviews over lunch. Although the applicant might regard this situation as less formal than the usual office interview, it may actually be more intimidating. The company representatives judge the candidate on many levels. Whether or not the candidate smokes, drinks, is aware of etiquette, or uses salt before tasting the food are actual considerations in some firms. (Pretaste salting, in some people's opinion, may indicate a dependence on habitual behavior rather than a willingness to assess a new situation and make decisions accordingly.)

Yet another technique is to envision the ideal applicant and seek a clone to replicate that vision. Such *benchmarking* works well, but not if the interviewer adheres too closely to the idealized image. There are many perfect candidates for any given job, and the candidates may differ radically in their backgrounds and experiences.

■ **Develop a definite plan for conducting the interview.**

An interview is essentially *a meeting* between you and the job applicant. And, as any good meeting leader knows, an agenda is essential for carrying out an efficient and timely meeting. The same is true of the interview meeting. Before you begin interviewing candidates, you must devise an agenda, or plan, that defines the stages of the interview and their sequence as well as the time allotted for each. In general, each plan should include the following stages:

- Greeting the applicant and putting him or her at ease with small talk

- Explaining to the candidate what you hope to accomplish with the interview

- Asking the candidate questions to draw out information about critical skills, personality traits, and other skills relevant to the job

- Describing the job

- Answering the applicant's questions (The best candidates, cognizant of their worth, will also be interviewing you!)

- Closing the interview and thanking the applicant

- Indicating to the applicant what the next step in the hiring process will be

> **"** When work is a pleasure, life
> is a joy! When work is duty,
> life is slavery. **"**
>
> —*Maxim Gorky*

1

Put the applicant at ease.

2

Avoid interview stereotypes.

3

Ensure that internal policies
are being followed.

4

Ensure that the questions you ask do
not violate Title VII of the Civil Rights
Act of 1964 or Title I of the Americans
with Disabilities Act of 1990.

5

Ask the right questions.

6

Give the applicant the opportunity
to ask questions of you.

7

End the interview on a positive,
professional note.

2

During the Employment Interview

A number of factors will govern what you say and do in the employment interview: internal policies, external regulations, the rules of common courtesy. Since the hiring decision you make based on the interview can have wide-ranging and significant ramifications on many lives, you must employ your finest skills of listening, assessing, asking, and deciding, while at the same time remaining within the confines of what is proper, polite, and legal!

Just as it is possible to "read between the lines," it is also possible to "listen between the lines." You will have to do both if you are to locate the right person for the job you are trying to fill. Recognize that resumé credentials do not necessarily equate with *capabilities:* a person may not have the exact experience or education you seek but, nonetheless, should be hired because of a fierce determination to work in your company. Listening well will enable you to hire well.

■ Put the applicant at ease.

Many candidates are nervous when they arrive for an interview. To create the best interview situation, you must put the candidate at ease. There are a number of ways to accomplish this:

- Select a room that is quiet.

- Do not permit interruptions from colleagues or from telephone calls.

- Allocate enough time for the interview and your subsequent record keeping.

- Sit beside the applicant rather than have a desk or table separate you.

- Remember that the applicant will probably be somewhat nervous. Offer a cup of coffee or a soft drink or a place to be seated, or engage in pleasantries such as "There's a fierce wind out there today, isn't there?" Explain to the applicant that you will be taking brief notes as he or she is speaking.

■ Avoid interview stereotypes.

No one ever said the interviewing process was easy. It isn't! It's hard—hard on both the interviewer *and* the interviewee. But it's a process that can lead to employment marriages made in heaven. One means of making the right match is to eliminate prejudicial thinking on your part—or at least to suspend it for the hour or two you will be conducting the interview. You must be honest enough and brave enough to analyze your own mind-sets or stereotypes and set them aside while you consider the factual information the candidate brings to the interview.

Not all well-dressed people will be hard-working employees. Not all people who are overweight are lazy. Not all blondes have an intelligence quotient lower than your own. Not all people less than six feet in height suffer from Napoleon complexes. A person with a physical disability may need an accommodation, but otherwise may be qualified to do the job. Some interviewers have a bias toward (and sometimes even a bias *against*) the well-educated candidate. Such interviewers look at the academic credentials of a candidate and decide that a person so well-educated must be very intelligent and, therefore, capable of handling any position. Sometimes, too, interviewers like to brag about the highly qualified candidates they have hired.

By contrast, other interviewers feel that an extensive educational background is detrimental, for it means the candidate has only theoretical knowledge and not hands-on experience. They may feel threatened by a person with these qualifications, or they may feel that such a candidate is overqualified and would soon leave the position.

As an interviewer, you must be cautious about letting stereotypical thinking interfere with your objective analysis of the candidate's overall fitness for the job. Education should be only one of numerous factors that constitute total suitability for the position. Using one of the interview forms in Appendix A enables you to avoid stereotypical thinking and disproportionately weighing a single aspect of the candidate's qualifications.

✍ Worksheet 3
Avoiding Interview Stereotypes

What are some stereotypes and related dangers that interviewers should be wary of? List some of the stereotypes. Then place a check in the box next to the ones closest to your style.

❏ The _____Candidate

The Danger:

_____

_____

_____

_____

❏ The _____Candidate

The Danger:

_____

_____

_____

_____

❏ The _____Candidate

The Danger:

_____

_____

_____

_____

❏ The _____Candidate

The Danger:

_____

_____

_____

_____

For suggestions, see Appendix C, page 114.

■ **Ensure that internal policies are being followed.**

Some companies have policies governing the way interviews should be conducted, including the type of information that should be presented (regarding salary, performance reviews, training, travel/relocation, probationary period, flex time, overtime, vacation, benefits), the parts of the building applicants should see, who the applicants should meet, and so forth. Some of these guidelines originate with the personnel department or with upper management. Be sure to consult with your own supervisor(s) and with the personnel department of your company to determine whether any such policies exist. Use the checklist in Appendix A to record the policies your company adheres to regarding interviews.

■ **Ensure that the questions you ask do not violate Title VII of the Civil Rights Act of 1964 or Title I of the Americans with Disabilities Act of 1990.**

Title VII of the Civil Rights Act of 1964, as amended, prohibits pre-employment inquiries that either directly or indirectly solicit information that may be used for discriminatory purposes. Some states even prohibit application questions that concern race, color, religion, sex, or national origin unless the employer is seeking such information to implement affirmative action programs.

Generally, the questions to be avoided deal with marital status, families, age and appearance, arrest and military discharge, and living arrangements. It is possible, of course, to tell the applicant that you will avoid specific, illegal questions, but explain that the applicant is welcome to share any job-relevant information. Be very careful about what you say and do during the interview. Even the most innocent or informal remarks may cause you and your firm legal problems.

Title I of the Americans with Disabilities Act of 1990 prohibits employers from discriminating against a qualified individual with a disability with respect to any employment decisions. Employers may not discriminate on the basis of disability in any aspect of the employment process, including application, testing, hiring, evaluation of assignments, disciplinary actions, training, promotion, medical exams, layoff/recall, termination, compensation, leave, and benefits.

Interview inquiries about whether an applicant has a disability or about the nature or severity of a disability are prohibited. Similarly, the applicant should not be asked about medical information, possible use of leave for medical reasons, or workers' compensation history.

Quick Tips . . .

Unfair Preemployment Inquiries

➤ Age
A question that suggests a preference for persons under 40 years of age.

➤ Arrests
All inquiries relating to arrests.

➤ Citizenship
Any inquiry about citizenship status. (It is fair to ask if the applicant can provide proof of citizenship, visa, or alien registration number after being hired.)

➤ Convictions
Questions that divulge conviction information not related to fitness to perform a particular job. Also unfair are questions not solely related to convictions or prison release within seven years of the date of job application.

➤ Family
Specific inquiries about the candidate's spouse, the spouse's employment or salary, children, child care arrangements, or dependents.

➤ Disabilities
It is unlawful to inquire whether an applicant has a disability or to ask about the nature or severity of the disability.

➤ Height/Weight
Any question not related to actual job requirements.

➤ Marital status
Inquiries related to applicant's marital status. Also unfair are checklists that ask the applicant to indicate a category representing marital status, such as Mr./Mrs./Miss.

➤ Military
Questions that ask about discharge; any request for discharge papers; an inquiry about the applicant's experience in other armed forces.

➢ Name   All inquiries about a name (or its origin)
                      that divulge marital status, lineage,
                      ancestry, national origin, or religion.

➢ National origin   Any inquiry concerning the applicant's
                      lineage, national origin, descent, birthplace,
                      or mother tongue. (The same kinds of
                      inquiries about the applicant's spouse are
                      also unfair.)

➢ Organizations   Any questions requiring the applicant to list
                      the organizations, clubs, societies, or other
                      similar groups to which he or she may belong.

➢ Photograph   Any request for a photograph prior to hiring.

➢ Pregnancy   All inquiries regarding pregnancy, including
                      medical history.

➢ Race or color   Inquiries that seek information about race
                      or color of skin, hair, etc.

➢ Relatives   Any inquiry about the names and addresses of
                      the candidate's relatives that might reveal
                      discriminatory information.

➢ Religion or creed   Questions about religious choices, including
                      holidays observed.

➢ Residence   Any inquiry about the names or relationship
                      of the applicant to persons with whom the
                      applicant resides; any inquiry that seeks to
                      learn whether the applicant owns a home.

➢ Sex   Any inquiry in this area is considered unfair.

✍ Worksheet 4
Employment Interview Script

As you read the following dialogue, use the space in the "Comments" column to record any of the interviewer's statements or questions that you feel are inappropriate, irrelevant, or clearly illegal. For simplicity in recording your comments and comparing them to the sample critique in Appendix C, pages 114 and 115, each paragraph is numbered.

Interview	Comments
1 **Mr. Jax:** Good morning, Susie. Just have a seat, here, next to the Kleenex box. I put the box here because I had an applicant who burst into tears this morning when I asked her about her children's health. It was so sad; her baby was stung by a killer bee and has had "hives"—no pun intended—ever since.	
2 **Susan Klem:** Good morning, Mr. Jax. I appreciate your taking the time to see me today. Your location here is beautiful.	
3 **Mr. Jax:** Yes, yes, it is. Now let's get started. I have another applicant coming in twenty minutes, so I'd like to get through this as quickly as possible. Let's see, I have your resumé someplace here. [He looks through the paper on his desk.] Klem . . . Klem . . . Klem—that's a German name, isn't it?	
4 **Susan Klem:** Actually, it's a Tasmanian name. I have another resumé here, if you want to use this one instead. [She hands it to him.]	

Interview	Comments
5 **Mr. Jax:** Thanks, Susie. By the way, do you prefer to be called Mrs. Klem?	
6 **Susan Klem:** Actually, it's Miss Klem, but you can call me Susie, if you like.	
7 **Mr. Jax:** It's been such a rough morning for me, Susie. My dog has ringworm, my wife is suffering with impacted teeth, my car's universal joint is disjointed, and my secretary just eloped. That's why I'm so disorganized. And that's why I need you. By the way, you don't have any mental or physical handicaps, do you?	
8 **Susan Klem:** Well, I was in an automobile accident last year and have had some lower back pain, but nothing serious.	
9 **Mr. Jax:** I don't even have a job description for you, but I can mail it to you afterwards. But tell me, do you have any questions about us here at Jax Crackers?	
10 **Susan Klem:** Actually, I do have a few questions, Mr. Jax. [He is reading her resumé as she is speaking.] I'd like to know exactly what the job entails, how it relates to the overall mission of the company, what opportunities there are for independent actions, and what the growth potential is for this position.	

Interview	Comments
11 Mr. Jax: Wow! You are well prepared aren't you? That's what I like—a girl with real initiative. And "front-office" appearance, too—if you know what I mean. [He winks to make sure she got the message.]	
Well, there really is a lot of growth potential in this position. And many opportunities for independence too. In fact, if you work weekends —Can you work on the weekends?—you will be in charge. In time, if Jax Crackers expands . . . [He is interrupted by a knock on the door.] Excuse me, Susie. Come in.	
12 Bill Pryze: Sorry to interrupt, Jack, but you asked me to stop by to meet the applicant for the secretarial job.	
13 Mr. Jax: It's no problem, Bill. I wanted you here. Sit down. I was just explaining to Susie here about the plans we have for expanding Jax Crackers and how that expansion would mean a promotion for her.	
14 Bill Pryze: We have projected opening new markets in the Pacific Rim as well as in three new domestic markets. Our projections include hiring four more secretaries within the next year. The person who is hired for this position will, in time, be in charge of those four other secretaries.	

Interview	Comments
Pardon me if I seem to be staring, but you look exactly like the valedictorian of our high school graduating class. You didn't happen to graduate from Ridgebury High in 1985, did you?	
15 **Susan Klem:** No, I graduated in 1980 from Edgerton High in Miami. Could you tell me a little more about the job?	
16 **Mr. Jax:** Actually, we can mail you all of that information. Right now, why don't you tell us a little more about yourself, since I have another applicant who will be walking through that door in about five minutes.	
What are your hobbies? What organizations do you belong to? What's your zodiac sign?	
17 **Susan Klem:** Well, I enjoy reading and taking classes. In fact, I just received my Secretarial Proficiency Certificate, and I've started taking business courses at the local community college. I'm also quite involved in church activities.	
18 **Mr. Jax:** Oh, what church is that? [The telephone on his desk rings. He picks it up and begins talking.]	
19 **Susan Klem:** [Five minutes later. She turns to Mr. Pryze.] Excuse me, Mr. Pryze, but I've decided that I do not wish to be considered as a candidate for this position. Would you please inform Mr. Jax when he is off the phone? And thank you for your time.	

Interview	Comments
20 **Mr. Jax:** [After he gets off the phone.] What happened, Bill? Where'd she go?	
21 **Bill Pryze:** She decided she didn't want the job after all.	
2 2 **Mr. Jax:** Jeepers. Creepers. Isn't that just like a woman? They can never make up thcir minds!	

■ Ask the right questions.

Ask the right questions during the interview in order to optimize the time expended by both you and the applicant. Poor questioning techniques lead to poor hiring choices. And poor hiring choices cost money!

Questions fall into one of two categories: *open-ended* and *close-ended.* Although close-ended questions are useful when you are trying to elicit specific information, as a rule, they should be avoided since they encourage monosyllabic responses that do not reveal in-depth information. Examples of close-ended questions are:

• How long did you work at Eastman Kodak?

• Have you taken any courses in accounting?

• Did you ever serve as a team leader?

• Have you had training in Total Quality Management?

Open-ended questions, on the other hand, allow the applicant to provide full responses. Responses to open-ended questions provide insights into many facets of the applicant's personality as well as reveal the applicant's qualifications. These are open-ended questions :

• How do you usually go about solving problems?

• In what ways have you improved processes?

• What are your views about achieving customer satisfaction?

As you can see, open-ended questions generally begin with words such as:

"What…?"
"Explain…"
"Describe…"
"How would you…?"
"In what ways…?"
"Under what circumstances do you…?"
"If you could…?"
"Please cite some examples of…"
"Tell me about…"

Open-ended questions allow you to draw out considerable information from the applicant, especially if you pause briefly after hearing the answer. Listen attentively to the responses so that you can ask subsequent questions directly related to earlier responses. If a candidate explains, for example, a preference for a given approach, you might ask, "What leads you to have that preference?" or "What experience have you had with the other approaches?"

Remember, however, that if you ask too many questions in rapid-fire succession, you may confuse the candidate or create a tense atmosphere. And you will probably only get back monosyllabic responses. Try to avoid predictable questions such as "What do you plan to be doing in five years?" Most savvy candidates are prepared for such questions and will have a polished answer for them. Instead, plan to ask at least a few unusual questions; you will find several on the list of General Interview Questions starting on page 21.

Also avoid asking *empty* questions. While these questions may be open-ended, if they are the wrong questions, you will waste your time asking them. Asking for an applicant's views on a recent movie may give you an idea of the applicant's cinematic taste, but it will do little to help you determine whether the candidate is qualified for the job—unless, of course, the job is in the film industry.

Using the right questions is simply a matter of practicing. And several practice exercises are included on the following pages. If you still can't seem to get the hang of it after completing the worksheets, write the questions you will use word-for-word on a sheet of paper and ask the questions, during the interview, exactly as they appear on that paper.

> " The highest art of professional management requires the literal ability to 'smell' a 'real fact' from all others. "
>
> —*Harold Geneen*

✍ Worksheet 5
Developing Open-Ended Questions

Try to convert the following close-ended questions to open-ended questions. Use the openings suggested on page 42. The first question has been done for you.

1. Do you get along well with others?

    Ask instead, "Can you give me an example that demonstrates how well you get along with others?"

2. Do you work well under pressure?

    Ask instead, _____

    _____

    _____

    _____

3. Are you a good problem-solver?

    Ask instead,_____

    _____

    _____

    _____

4. Do you consider yourself a quick learner?

    Ask instead,_____

    _____

    _____

    _____

5. How long have you worked as a purchasing agent?
    Ask instead,_____

    _____

    _____

    _____

6. Are you a creative person?

    Ask instead,_____

    _____

    _____

    _____

7. Have you made changes that substantially improved the process on which you were working?

    Ask instead,_____

    _____

    _____

    _____

8. Do you like having responsibilities?

    Ask instead,_____

    _____

    _____

    _____

9. Can you organize things?

    Ask instead,_____

    _____

    _____

    _____

10. Are you satisfied with the work you do?

    Ask instead,_____

    _____

    _____

    _____

For suggestions, see Appendix C, page 116.

✍ Worksheet 6
Identifying Question Types

In the space preceding each question, write the letter that identifies the kind of question.

Y/N = Yes-No   C = Close-ended   L = Leading   E = Empty

_____   1. You probably really enjoy working with children, don't you?

_____   2. So, it says here on your resumé that you went to the University of Rochester. Didn't you hate the winters there?

_____   3. Have you always wanted to be a teacher?

_____   4. How many computer courses have you taken?

_____   5. You wouldn't mind working overtime occasionally, would you?

_____   6. Have you finished all your Christmas shopping?

_____   7. How long did you work at Parkbrook Hospital?

_____   8. Do you enjoy accounting work?

_____   9. There is a great deal of public contact in this job. How well do you relate to external customers?

_____   10. That's a gorgeous brooch you are wearing. Where did you ever find it?

For suggestions, see Appendix C, page 116.

■ **Give the applicant the opportunity to ask questions of you.**

As a rule, the closer the position is to the executive level, the greater the likelihood that the applicant will have questions for you, the interviewer. No matter what the position, though, many applicants believe that life is too short to be wasted on a job that does not bring them satisfaction. And satisfaction is often defined in words that include more than monetary considerations.

Successful interviewing depends as much on your finding the right applicant as the applicant finding the right job. If the interview situation does not result in a win-win outcome, both parties will be losers. You should feel, when you are through with the interviews, that you have selected the best possible person for the job. And the person who is selected should feel that your company offers exactly what he or she is seeking in terms of a fulfilling job. In order to feel that way, however, the applicant will need to ask you some questions.

Some of the questions that applicants frequently ask are:

* What is your company's mission?
* Could you describe the person I will be working for?
* Please tell me a little about the others who have held this position. Were they promoted? Did they quit? Were they transferred?
* What would be the worst mistake I could make if I held this job?
* How much opportunity does this job provide for self-governing work?

■ **End the interview on a positive, professional note.**

The applicant has invested considerable time and often money preparing to tell you why he or she deserves to be hired for the job you have available. The true professional is aware of the energy the applicant has expended and appreciates the applicant's efforts. As you prepare to close the interview, ask whether the candidate has any questions or would like to share any further information with you.

At this point, when the interview is virtually complete, the applicant may ask you to comment on how well he or she did. Be diplomatic but honest. Do not mislead applicants who don't have the qualifications you are seeking. On the other hand, if an applicant seems to be an obvious choice, do not make any commitments, as you will still have to check references and probably confer with others regarding your choice. Above all, do not make any commitments or promises at this point, particularly about salary, promotions, or pay raises.

To close the interview, explain to the applicant what will happen next and approximately how long it will take you to make a decision. Then thank the candidate for meeting with you.

> **"Thou, O God, dost sell us all good things at the price of labor."**
>
> —*Leonardo da Vinci*

Success Strategies From...

Babak Robert Nabati, President, Baron Property Development

On Hiring: "Honesty and loyalty are the two most sought-after qualities when hiring prospective employees. Experience, a candid and probing interview (during which the interviewer must avoid facile assumptions and instead pose cogent questions to the applicant), and a sixth sense are often the only tools by which to judge whether the applicant has the stuff to become an honest, loyal, and productive employee.

"Since many people believe job-hopping is a national sport in America, it is important to make the workplace one that inspires loyalty in the worker...

"It's important to determine that the applicant truly wants and needs that job...

"Ultimately, of course, the process is always somewhat of a gamble. Yet, fairness and true professionalism in your treatment of those who work for you are the best ways to bring out the best in employees. The gambling continues, but at least the odds are in your favor."

1

Document your evaluation
of the candidate.

2

Make your decision and notify
the candidates who were not selected.

3

Conduct a reference check on the
applicant(s) you have chosen.

4

Invite candidate(s) back for
a second interview.

5

After you have made your final
choice, officially notify the candidate
and schedule the proper
orientation program.

3

After the Employment Interview

■ Document your evaluation of the candidate.

Even if you have another applicant waiting, you should take a few minutes to record your impressions of the candidate you have just interviewed. Document the applicant's ability to perform the essential functions of the job or what, if any, reasonable accommodations may need to be made. Do not make notes concerning personal appearance or perceived disabilities. Criteria for your notes should be job-related and consistently recorded for each applicant being interviewed.

It is surprising (but not to anyone who has done extensive interviewing) how hard it is afterwards to remember who was who. Your next step is to use one of the interview forms printed in Appendix A to assess the candidate's strengths and weaknesses.

Make your assessment quickly; don't deliberate or agonize over the allocation of points. Tally the numbers, make a few additional notes, and jot down a quick critique of your own interviewing skills, using the Interviewer Self-Assessment Form in Appendix A. You will become an efficient and successful interviewer, in time, if you are continually refining your own interviewing skills.

All these documentation steps, by the way, should take no more than five minutes. Build in that five-minute period at the end of each interview as you schedule your interviewing day.

■ Make your decision and notify the candidates who were not selected.

Once all the interviews have been conducted, decide which applicant is best for the job. Next, as a professional courtesy, you should notify each candidate who was eliminated. Although you may find this difficult, if you use a form letter such as the one in Figure 5, it should take only a few moments to notify these individuals. Remember to begin the notification process immediately because many of the people you interviewed may be postponing decisions about other job opportunities or career moves while waiting to hear your decision.

123 First Street
Anytown, Ohio 00000
March, 1991

Dear Mr. Jones:

Thank you for taking the time recently to come in for an interview for the position of budget analyst at the ABC Widget Company. I enjoyed talking with you and learning about your background.

We had a large number of candidates apply for this job. All of them, like yourself, had a great deal to offer. One applicant, however, who had the combination of background, education, experience, and skills that matched the job requirements exactly, has been hired to fill this position.

Be assured that we will keep your resumé on file so that you can be considered should a future opening occur that calls for your talents. We wish you the best of luck in your job search.

Sincerely,

Mary Smith
Personnel Director

Fig. 5.   Candidates who are eliminated or are no longer being considered for a position should be notified as soon as possible.

■ Conduct a reference check on the applicant(s) you have chosen.

Because lawsuits abound in our society today, employers are becoming cautious about their statements regarding former employees. In fact, many companies will only verify vital statistics such as the length of time the employee worked and the salary earned.

Nonetheless, it is important that you contact at least five references, with at least two of those references being former employers. Of course, you should only contact references the candidate has listed.

You may wish to use a form like the Telephone Reference Check Sheet in Appendix A for your telephone reference checks. If you have narrowed your choice to two or three applicants, you should make the same inquiries about each candidate.

■ Invite candidate(s) back for a second interview.

Depending upon a number of factors, including time, the nature of the position, the number of final candidates, and corporate policy, you may wish to call your finalist(s) back for a second interview. Additional company representatives are often included in this second interview. The selection of these additional people may be made by you, your boss, upper management, the personnel department, or even the department in which the newly hired person will work.

No matter who is present, however, this second interview gives you the opportunity to ask questions that are even more specific, even more penetrating than the first round of questions were. The initial interview was an opportunity to separate this candidate from the groups of other candidates, to define his or her attributes in comparison to others.

This second interview is more of an opportunity *to refine*. You will attempt to ensure that this person will fit well into the department and represent the company well. Introducing the candidate to the individuals with whom he or she will work, if chosen, is an appropriate action at this time. You may also wish to ask other questions that occurred to you after the first interview, perhaps as you made notes or as the references were giving you information. *Never repeat, however, any information that was given to you by the references.* You may formulate questions based on information that was shared with you, but you will find yourself in serious trouble if you ask a question such as: "When I called Mr. Johnson at XYZ Company, he told me you have a problem getting to work on time. How do you respond to that charge?"

The applicant may respond by filing a lawsuit for defamation of character!

> **"** Few managers will deny that they are only as good as the people they hire. What is hard to believe is the haphazard way they actually go about filling openings in their territories. Getting somebody, almost *anybody*, is more often than not the driving force in field sales staffing. One manager summed it up graphically when he said, 'Bad breath is better than no breath.' **"**
>
> — *Jack Falvey*

■ **After you have made your final choice, officially notify the candidate and schedule the proper orientation program.**

If, after this second or third interview, you still have reservations about the candidate, you may have to begin the entire hiring process again. Or, you may wish to consider applicants who were eliminated from the first selection round.

But, assuming you find the most suitable candidate for the position, officially notify that person by telephone or by mail. If you do send an official letter, make it warm and welcoming, but also make it a carefully worded, semilegal document that restates the agreed-upon terms of employment. Specify the job title, the salary, the benefits such as vacation time, and any prerequisites that accompany the position. Cite the date on which the candidate will be expected to report to work.

The official letter may also cite expectations the company has for the employee or the position, or its corporate mission, or even the kinds of conduct that are considered grounds for dismissal. Many firms

MEMO

To: All Members of the Accounting Department

From: C.R. Cranston, Department Head

Re: Tim Allen, Newly Hired Budget Analyst

Please help me welcome Tim Allen, who has been hired to fill the position of Budget Analyst. Tim is a graduate of the Rochester Institute of Technology and brings a wealth of experience, including five years in the U.S. General Accounting Office and four years as a certified public accountant in the Mitchell and Langley accounting firm.

He begins work on Monday, March 11. Please join me in welcoming Tim to ABC.

Thank you.

Fig. 6.   Once a person has been hired for a position, circulate to other staff members a memo announcing the new employee.

have actual employment contracts, particularly for higher level positions. In service industries, these contracts usually stipulate that for a given period of time following a person's resignation or dismissal, the person cannot work for the clients of the former employer.

Then proceed to arrange the usual orientation for new employees. You should also put out a brief memo to the members of the department in which the new employee will be working. A sample memo is shown in Figure 6.

Summary

Before the Employment Interview

- Decide how you will find the person to fill the position.
- Determine the qualities and skills you wish the candidate to have and revise, update, or create a job description identifying the essential functions of the job.
- Prepare a list of questions that you will ask of each candidate.
- Take notes and prepare a form to use in assessing applicants.
- Choose an interview style.
- Develop a definite plan for conducting the interview.

During the Employment Interview

- Put the applicant at ease.
- Avoid interview stereotypes.
- Ensure that internal policies are being followed.
- Ensure that the questions you ask do not violate Title VII of the Civil Rights Act of 1964 or Title I of the Americans with Disabilities Act of 1990.
- Ask the right questions.
- Give the applicant the opportunity to ask questions of you.
- End the interview on a positive, professional note.

After the Employment Interview

- Document your evaluation of the candidate.
- Make your decision and notify the candidates who were not selected.
- Conduct a reference check on the applicant(s) you have chosen.
- Invite candidate(s) back for a second interview.
- After you have made your final choice, officially notify the candidate and schedule the proper orientation program.

2

The Firing Process

Introduction

Few people can go through a lifetime of employment without being fired at least once. As heart-wrenching and ulcer-producing as that process often is, it need *not* be. In fact, if properly handled, the termination meeting can be the springboard that allows the employee to escape a confining job and seek a more rewarding one.

Many people are subsequently grateful they were fired, for their new jobs—which they would probably never have found had they not been fired—allow them to grow and to demonstrate leadership and to earn more money than they had been earning. In fact, when a group of individuals who had just been fired were surveyed, 75 percent of them described the process as "the worst thing that ever happened to them." And yet, when those same individuals were interviewed again a year later, the majority said that the firing was "the best thing that ever happened."

The termination process can be painless if we keep in mind one simple fact: termination just means that the person being terminated is in the wrong job. It does *not* mean that the person is inadequate or stupid or lazy or any one of a hundred other negative adjectives. Firing just means the person now has an opportunity to find the job for which he or she is best suited.

Studies of millionaires, for example, have found that they quit or were fired from at least twelve jobs before finding the line of work that proved to be remarkably successful for them. Lee Iacocca is a perfect example of someone whose firing led to a new job that brought international recognition, a million-aire status, and a place in the history books.

America is a huge land and, quite literally, the land of opportunity. There are hundreds of other jobs out there, jobs that will bring greater opportunities and satisfaction than the one the terminated individual held. Of course, such future-oriented opportunity may not be very consoling to the person about to lose a job. It is up to you, the termination interviewer, to assure the person that your decision is the best one for all concerned.

You can fire a person and make that person feel devastated, hopeless, worth-less. You can strip the person of dignity. You can evoke such anger that the

59

person retaliates for the harsh or humiliating treatment. Sadly, we have all probably read stories about fired individuals who returned to their former workplace and sought revenge against those they felt had been unfair to them.

Be assured that while firing is an admittedly difficult process, it can be a positive process, one that allows the person being fired to find a more satisfying job. The process can also allow the firm to find another employee whose interests and talents are more aligned to the job requirements. Firing really can have win-win results.

Individual Firings vs. Downsizing. More and more employers are struggling to create those win-win situations, whether the terminations are the result of *individual firings* or *downsizing*, the two most common termination situations. Firing usually involves a single individual who has failed to perform satisfactorily. Downsizing usually involves a great many people company-wide, whose terminations are the result of economic factors unrelated to their performance. Firing may be called dismissal, demotion, enforced resignation, or termination. Downsizing may be called destaffing, dehiring, decentralization, pyramid-flattening, belt-tightening, derecruiting, laying off, reducing manpower, enhancing the efficiency of operations, taking appropriate cost reduction actions, or eliminating redundancies in the human resource area. No matter what it is called, no matter what the rationale behind it, separating individuals from their source of a livelihood is a painful process.

In the case of downsizing, employees who once worked with discharged employees may experience fear, lower morale, and lessened productivity in the wake of finding that their work unit has been reduced. The organizational leaders, managers, and supervisors alike must work especially hard in such times to assure the remaining employees that the company will do all it can to protect employee interests. With widespread layoffs, it is better to keep employees informed about the worst possible scenario than to pretend that no changes will be made. It is always easier to deal with the known—even if it is not favorable—than to deal with the unknown.

With firing situations, the manager should strive to show appreciation of the remaining employees' work in order to assure them that they are not in the same position as the discharged employee was. Certainly, it is unprofessional to discuss the circumstances that led to the discharge, but it is professional to praise employees for the work they are doing. By doing this, the manager can avoid discussing the circumstances of the firing and still make employees aware that the company values their contributions.

When economic conditions force corporations to reduce their work force numbers, decisions must be made concerning the most equitable way to make the cuts. Ideally, the decisions will be made after extensive input from several key figures in the company. Here are some of the ways that organizations make the necessary cuts:

- *Eliminate a whole department or work group.* In the manufacturing realm, for example, if a prototype has been developed by a work unit and then the prototype is not accepted by the customer, the whole prototype group may be out of a job.

- *Make across-the-board cuts of a certain percentage.* According to professional development specialist Brenda Avadian, one of the problems with this approach is that some departments may have large enough staffs that even if a few positions were eliminated, the remaining employees could get the work done with little problem while other departments may have been operating on a "mean-and-lean" basis already. Across-the-board reductions can create real inequities.

- *Allow natural attrition losses (from retirement, death, or resignation) to create smaller work groups.* However, if the remaining team members are expected to do the work of the lost member without receiving any additional recompense for the additional work, a serious morale problem may result.

- *Encourage early retirement.* While the company may have to entice older workers via generous retirement packages, or "golden parachutes," the company will save money in the long run by being able to hire younger, less expensive workers.

- *Put a freeze on hiring.* In times of economic recession, when firms are expected to do more with less, companies may put a temporary hold on bringing in new employees.

- *Ask for voluntary efforts from the work force.* Some companies have found that in hard times, employees are willing to reduce their work hours, postpone pay increases, relocate, or switch from full-time to part-time status.

- *Involve experts.* As early in the downsizing process as possible, firms should involve representatives from each layer of the organization, including union representatives. The goal of the decision-making group would be to define the need—general or specific, long-range or short-range—and to implement the fairest, most humane way of reducing the work force. Corporate reorganization may be the answer—so may a thorough analysis of key positions to determine their true value to the company. In the face of extensive layoffs, many companies hire outplacement firms to aid about-to-be-discharged employees with the job-hunting process.

In the pages that follow, we will consider the microcosmic, one-on-one dismissal situation rather than the corporate decision to lay off thousands of employees. Most managers find they need more help with firm, but humane, dismissals than with large manpower reductions.

Quick Tips...

Downsizing Methods

➤ Eliminate a whole department or work group.

➤ Make across-the-board cuts of a certain percentage.

➤ Allow natural attrition to create smaller work groups.

➤ Encourage early retirement.

➤ Put a freeze on hiring.

➤ Ask employees to postpone wage increases, switch from full-time to part-time, or relocate.

➤ Seek expert advice for implementing cuts in the least painful way possible.

Success Strategies From...

Victor Ciaccia, Vice President of AVS Lettering, Inc., Rochester, New York

"Due to the current economic climate, small businesses, like big businesses, are forced to consider layoffs. In a small business, however, letting go of three people could mean a 50 percent reduction in staff. We try to meet with the individual we have to terminate and advise that his or her position has been targeted for staff reduction. Prior to such a meeting, we will have made all employees aware of the anticipated need to make significant cuts. The primary vehicle we use to share such information is the staff meeting."

Ciaccia offers these suggestions for easing the transition for employees who are affected by such cutbacks:

- Emphasize that the cut does not in any way reflect performance.

- Express appreciation for the employees' loyalty and commitment to the company.

- If possible, provide time off with pay during a two-week period, during which the employees are free to seek employment elsewhere.

- Offer letters of recommendation and personal references.

- Grant the opportunity to leave for new employment prior to the stipulated termination date.

- Assure employees that consideration will be given to rehiring them if and when the economic climate improves.

1

Maintain an open dialogue with the employee who may be having trouble. Begin the process informally.

2

Make the meetings and your recordkeeping more formal if the problem persists.

3

Protect yourself and your company against wrongful discharge lawsuits.

4

Before the Termination Meeting

No matter what we call it, firing is often a painful process for both the supervisor and the employee. The earlier you detect the employee's job-related problems, the sooner you can offer counseling to help solve the problem. People are fired for only two reasons—poor performance and poor relations with others. Check the list of warning signs on page 67 for behaviors that indicate that an employee may be having difficulty in one or both of these areas.

The termination meeting may never come about if you follow certain steps. When you notice the warning signals, you need to step in and begin an open, informal dialogue with the employee who is having trouble. When problems are "nipped in the bud," they usually do not escalate to the level of a termination meeting.

Sometimes, however, terminating an employee is necessary. As with most things in life, success (or, in this case, achieving a win-win situation) comes to those who have prepared for it. If your performance management meetings are to yield optimal results, they must be carefully thought out. Here are some steps to follow before the firing (and subsequent exit interview) takes place.

■ **Maintain an open dialogue with the employee who may be having trouble. Begin the process informally.**

The good supervisor will spot trouble before it erupts. If the hiring process was a thorough one, chances are the individual and the job are aligned. However, you may have "inherited" an employee you did not hire and who is, perhaps, in the wrong position.

The sooner you spot the discrepancy between the employee's performance and your expectations for the position, the more readily you can minimize the discrepancy. Communication is the key. Talk informally to the individual who seems to be having problems. Learn what is troubling that person. Make a few notes during this informal meeting so that you can more easily pursue the appropriate course of action. For example, if the employee expresses a feeling of being "in over his head," the problem may be inadequate training. The solution: Arrange for the employee to receive the needed training.

> **"Downsizing has become an organizational activity, often independent of economic growth or contraction."**
>
> —*American Management Association*

Even if you do not have the necessary funds, there are many ways you can provide the additional training without spending a single penny. Use Worksheet 7 on page 68 to brainstorm some of those ways.

An on-the-job problem may simply be the result of a temporary alteration of the employee's usual state, particularly at home. Perhaps the employee is not feeling well, has a sick child or an ailing parent, or has been taking night courses and is worried about a final exam. You have no right to pry into an employee's private life. You do, however, have the right to discuss a change you perceive in the employee's usual good performance. One way to broach the delicate subject would be with a question such as this: "George, I've noticed that you are not your usual, energetic self. And your work seems to be suffering a little as a result. I'm a little worried about you. Is there anything I can help you with?"

Quick Tips...

Warning Signs for Job-Related Problems

➤ Turns work in late; misses deadlines

➤ Has petty conflicts with co-workers

➤ Produces less

➤ Does not make contributions in meetings

➤ Is frequently late

➤ Is frequently absent

➤ Spends too much time on the telephone

➤ Takes long breaks

➤ Is reluctant to change

➤ Seems isolated or unhappy

➤ "Flies off the handle"

➤ Does not volunteer for assignments

➤ Is not invited to join co-workers in social activities

✍ Worksheet 7
Identifying Training Methods

Use the space below to record the ways you can provide your
employees with additional job training at little or no cost.

_____

_____

_____

_____

_____

_____

_____

_____

_____

_____

_____

_____

_____

_____

_____

_____

_____

_____

_____

_____

See Appendix C, page 117, for suggested training methods.

✍ Worksheet 8
Developing Opening Dialogues
With Problem Employees

What are some diplomatic openings that would encourage an employee to discuss underlying causes of poor work performance?

_____

_____

_____

_____

_____

_____

_____

_____

_____

_____

_____

_____

_____

_____

_____

_____

_____

_____

_____

_____

_____

_____

_____

_____

■ **Make the meetings and your recordkeeping more formal if the problem persists.**

If the problem cannot be resolved informally, or if it is more deep-rooted or long-term than you initially believed, you may have to move to the next stage: counseling the employee and reaching an agreement regarding the employee's intentions to improve the situation.

It may be that the individual is not doing the job due to insufficient training. This is an easy situation to remedy. If the employee continues to make mistakes and perform poorly after the training period, it may be that the person simply cannot, or will not, do what is expected.

If the latter is the case, your disciplinary meetings will need to become more formal and more stringent. Because these meetings are more serious, you should keep more detailed records. When interacting with an employee at this stage, it is important to remember the course the meeting should take:

• Begin with a specific description of what you feel the problem is.

• Next, permit the employee to explain his or her perspective of the problem you have described.

• Discuss what can be done to correct the problem and work out a mutual agreement regarding the next steps to be taken. Formalize the agreement with a handshake. Also put the agreement in writing and give a copy to the employee as soon as possible.

• Follow through by periodically monitoring the employee's efforts to carry out the arrangement.

Remember that at this point in the disciplinary process, there is still time and room for improvement. You will continue to coach and to help the individual meet the goals established during the disciplinary meetings. As you plan for these meetings, you may find the Discipline Form in Appendix B useful. Note that the word "discipline" is being used in its most positive sense. This form is to be used for "disciplining" employees—for helping them to acquire discipline, not for being punitive with them. Just as an outstanding athlete is a disciplined individual, so, too, is a good employee. You could say that a disciplined employee is one whose work is efficient and orderly and in keeping with expected rules of conduct. Following are some suggestions for making the disciplinary meetings as painless as possible.

Be prepared with a plan of action. Anticipate the employee's response and have your answers ready.

Give advance notice of the meeting so the employee can also be prepared. Advise the employee of the amount of time you expect the meeting to take. Don't set the meeting too far in advance and prolong the employee's anxiety.

Avoid interruptions during the meeting; do not permit distractions. Make certain you are meeting in a private, not a public, place. What transpires during this meeting is of critical importance and potentially embarrassing for the employee. Extend the employee every possible professional courtesy.

Begin with pleasantries but not humor. This is not a light situation, so you should keep the tone businesslike, yet not harsh. Make the atmosphere as comfortable as possible.

Cite your earlier informal discussions about the employee's problem. Indicate that you are documenting this meeting and any future discipline meetings, which will increase in seriousness.

State the problem clearly. Be impartial. Use facts, not rumors or impressions. Try not to be judgmental or evaluative; use facts in your statements. Instead of saying, "You are always late," say "You were late to work four times in the last two weeks."

Avoid absolute words such as "always," "never," and "inevitably."

Explain your objective for the meeting. Likewise, encourage the employee to state his or her objectives. Relate the objectives to the corporate goals and mission. Throughout the disciplinary meeting, make every effort to keep the discussion aligned with your ultimate intent, which is to create the best circumstances for the organization. Ideally, those circumstances will include an employee who has changed his or her behavior to meet job expectations and feels satisfaction in doing so. However, if the employee is unable or unwilling to make such shifts, dismissing the employee is probably the best course of action.

Everyone is motivated. Your employee may not be motivated to achieve your objectives, but the employee is motivated, nonetheless, to do some things. *Try to learn what does motivate the employee* and work to make that motivational influence part of his or her job environment.

Make it clear that your concern is for both the individual and the group. Be sincere. Attempt to make the employee understand your position and your responsibility to do what is in the best interests of the organization.

Be aware of theatrics. Some employees will display dramatic behavior to get you to overlook their behavior or broken promises. Be prepared for tears, shouting, loud voices, accusations, or attempts to blame you or others. Of course, you must be able to separate theatrics from real anger. If the situation becomes volatile, you must defuse it before actual rage erupts. It may help to ask another person, such as a union representative, to be present. Or, you may want to suggest a change: perhaps the meeting could be continued later or perhaps you could interrupt the flow of events by arranging for a coffee break.

Maintain eye contact with the employee. Give no indication that you are uncomfortable or, worse yet, afraid. You may need to practice several times until you reach the point where your composure is evident in both your words and your actions.

Don't be led astray. An employee may attempt to sidetrack you with statements such as "Everybody else does the same thing. Why are you picking on me?" Do not allow the employee to draw you into making comparisons to other employees. Insist on dealing with the problem employee's behavior rather than the behavior of other employees.

Be specific. Give actual examples from the work situation. Be deliberate and purposeful in your selection of work-related incidents that demonstrate the unsatisfactory behavior. Clearly, you will need to compile carefully detailed records during the weeks that precede each discipline meeting.

Do not rely on rumors. Stick to the facts, as you perceive them. Ask the employee whether the facts you cite are correct. Give the employee an opportunity to present his or her side. If the employee needs more time to gather other facts, agree to postpone the meeting to a later time.

Ask for feedback. Listen carefully to the employee's explanations. Don't interrupt. Do not present too much information all at once. Allow the individual time to respond to each of the "charges" you make.

Keep the discussion on target. Stay focused. Keep your objective in the forefront of the discussion. Prepare an outline, if necessary, and show it to the employee before the meeting begins. Refer to it several times during the course of the meeting.

Don't apologize. You are, after all, only doing your job. If you have been fair in your documentation, if you have treated the individual with respect, and if your actions have been prompted by the sincere desire to help the individual, you have nothing to be sorry for.

Be aware of your body language.

Maintain control of the situation. While you want it to be a two-way discussion, you must be the one to lead and direct that discussion. Yes, you will elicit the employee's opinions or suggestions and you will try to actively involve the employee in the proposed plan of action, but do not permit the employee to formulate that plan.

Stress the positive. Don't permit the situation to become negative. Point out the contributions the person has made to the company. After all, the employee was hired because of specific talents, and if the employee has been on the job for a period of time, he or she must have been doing more good than bad or he or she would probably have been fired long before this. Don't be too positive, though, particularly in the later discipline meetings, when the consequences for noncompliance will be more severe. You don't want to confuse the issue or the employee. If you are too complimentary, the employee may wonder why the discipline meeting is necessary!

Stay calm. If you find yourself getting "hot under the collar," breathe deeply and change the pace of the conversation. Rather than speak extemporaneously, change the topic, excuse yourself to get a cup of coffee, or refer to your documentation.

Sometimes it helps to reverse roles. You might try asking what the employee would do if he or she were you. The answer may be one that you can live with.

Do not make promises. Rather, aim to reach an agreement that establishes checkpoint dates by which you and the employee can confer to see how well the terms of the agreement are being met. Put the agreement in writing, and give a copy to the employee as soon as possible after the meeting.

Quick Tips . . .

Disciplining Without Tears

➢ Have a plan of action ready.

➢ Advise the employee of the meeting in advance.

➢ Avoid interruptions and don't permit distractions.

➢ Begin on a pleasant note.

➢ Cite earlier discussions of the employee's problem.

➢ State the problem clearly.

➢ Avoid using absolutes.

➢ Explain the meeting's objective.

➢ Find out what motivates the employee.

➢ State that you are trying to do what is best for all concerned.

➢ Be aware of theatrics.

➢ Maintain eye contact.

➢ Don't let the employee sidetrack you.

➢ Give specific examples from actual work situations when discussing the employee's problem.

➢ Don't rely on rumors.

➢ Ask for feedback.

➢ Keep the discussion on target.

➢ Don't apologize.

➢ Be aware of your body language.

➢ Maintain control of the situation.

➢ Stress the positive.

➢ Stay calm.

➢ Reverse roles with the employee.

➢ Don't make promises.

End the meeting with a handshake and a mention of when the next meeting will occur. Give your pledge to help the employee follow the plan of action that has been agreed upon. Elicit a similar pledge from the employee.

Thank the employee for meeting with you and for showing a willingness to cooperate.

After five disciplinary meetings and a progression from oral reprimands to written notice, it is time to consider the termination meeting if the person still shows no sign of improvement.

To be entirely sure that terminating the employee is the best course of action, fill out the Pretermination Questionnaire in Appendix B. Among the questions you must consider at this point are:

- The employee's work record prior to the recent period of difficulty.

- The source of the problem: personality conflict vs. inability to do the work.

- The overall treatment of the employee, including whether the employee was given ample opportunity to improve, whether the employee's side was heard, whether the employee was given adequate tools and training for doing the job.

- The severity of the present disciplinary actions vs. that of actions taken for similar situations that occurred in the past.

- The consequences of firing the employee.

If you do decide that termination is necessary, check with the necessary corporate personnel to ensure that you have followed proper termination procedures. Then during the termination meeting, you can speak with authority, letting the employee know that you have alerted the proper individuals and that the decision is final. (Some employees feel they can win back their jobs by going over their supervisor's head to plead with a higher executive.)

You must be careful to adhere to the proper termination procedures to protect both yourself and your company from wrongful discharge lawsuits.

■ **Protect yourself and your company against wrongful discharge lawsuits.**

The discharge meeting, as we've said, can be a win-win situation. Or, it can be handled so poorly that negative consequences follow. Those negative consequences might be physical abuse against the supervisor doing the discharging, subsequent badmouthing of the company by the disgruntled employee, or expensive litigation.

About-to-be-fired employees are usually not surprised to learn they will be fired. In fact, many of them believe they deserve to be fired and are eager to break away and start a new job. Keeping an employee who is performing poorly is unfair to all concerned—to the employee who is wasting time in a job for which he or she is probably ill-suited; to co-workers who can see that the employee is not working up to company standards; and to you as the supervisor, who must expend the time trying to make the employee perform according to standards.

You must, of course, keep carefully documented records, tracking meetings you had with the employee in the past and tracking the causes for the dismissal decision you have made. You *must* keep records on all employees, however; otherwise, you may be faced with a lawsuit that says you were discriminating against the dismissed employee.

Lawsuits are on the rise—for all kinds of reasons. As a representative of your firm, you make the firm liable for your own improper actions, even those you may commit unknowingly.

Because there is no one law that covers all workplace situations, managers must remain in close contact with the legal counsel retained by the firm whenever questionable situations arise. There are a plethora of federal and state rulings, various employment contracts, union regulations, handbook policies, and diverse corporate practices that govern the complex decisions about what is right in the workplace. Since your words and actions could have extensive ramifications, you must retain an attorney to help you interpret both the state and federal laws, which are amended over the years as new precedents are set. Conformance to the requirements of the Civil Rights Act of 1964, the Americans with Disabilities Act of 1990, and the Equal Employment Opportunity Act of 1972 (Public Law 92-261) will minimize the need for employees to seek redress through legal means. Abiding by the laws is in the best interests of *both* employee and employer. Even if your company is able to prove in court that it acted properly, the process of gathering and then presenting that proof is expensive. Here are suggestions that will help protect you and your organization against wrongful discharge suits:

- Recognize that courts may be sympathetic to the litigant who is battling against a corporate adversary. They may also lean toward the discharged employee who was treated in a harsh or humiliating manner, particularly if no reason was given for dismissal. If the employee has an outstanding and long employment record and performance appraisals have consistently been commendable, the company will have a harder time proving the correctness of its actions.

- Prior to the meeting, plan what you will say. During the discharge meeting, do not use value judgment terms like "irresponsible," "lazy," or "dishonest." Instead, rely on factual records: the person was late seventeen times or called in sick thirty-two times. Do not mock or humiliate the person. You may wish to use a tape recorder and let the employee know you are doing so. Of course, if you do record the meeting, you must be absolutely certain to follow the proper course of action. Write out a script and rehearse it.

- You may wish, if you anticipate a potentially difficult situation, to have corporate counsel be part of the termination meeting. Arrange schedules in advance.

- Plan to keep the meeting short. The longer it is, the more likely you are to say something you will later regret and the more painful it will probably be for the discharged employee. Set a time limit and stick to it.

- Make certain the firing conditions have been made known, repeatedly, to all employees. Those conditions should be spelled out when the person is first hired. As soon as you suspect a performance problem, repeat the conditions which, if violated, could lead to dismissal. Employment contracts will substantiate your defense.

- Anticipate the antisexism, antiageism, antiracism mood of the country and do not fire employees for reasons that will lead to charges of sexism, ageism, or racism. For example, firing a woman who does not wear makeup will probably cost you more than just legal expenses. The media attention alone your firm will receive will make you regret your decision.

- Make certain that you conduct regular performance reviews, not only the regularly scheduled appraisal meeting, but also several progress meetings. Put your assessments in writing and have the employee sign a statement that he or she has been given this information, even if he or she does not agree with it.

- Do not make promises or threats, at any time. Promises of job security during an employment interview have led to litigation. Threats made in the heat of the moment have had similar consequences. Throughout the counseling period, as you attempt to help the employee meet your performance expectations, keep the employee apprised of the logical, rational steps that will be followed in the process of helping him or her meet those standards.

- Do not terminate or fire employees for reasons that will lead to charges of discrimination based on a physical or mental disability; for example, firing an employee because he or she is undergoing counseling and is taking medication for depression. The New Civil Rights Act of 1991 amends the Americans with Disabilities Act of 1990 by providing substantial monetary awards to victims of employment discrimination.

> **❝ If you aren't fired with enthusiasm, you will be fired with enthusiasm. ❞**
>
> *—Vince Lombardi*

✍ Worksheet 9
Avoiding Wrongful Discharge Suits: Four Case Studies

Decide who you would have sided with in each of the following cases. Then turn to Appendix C to see whether your decision matched the court's ruling. These cases are included not as an offering of legal advice, but to stress the importance of being cautious about your own managerial actions and the actions of your other employees.

Case Study 1

An employee was told by his boss to put leaded gas in a company vehicle. The employee spoke up and asked the boss whether they should be using unleaded, as the signs on the vehicle urged. The boss interpreted the employee's question as insubordination and told the employee to either do what was ordered or look for another job.

The employee looked for an attorney instead and brought the matter to court. You be the judge. Would you have upheld the company, which felt the employee was a troublemaker who refused to follow orders, or would you have ruled for the employee, who felt that he had been asked to violate a law? Explain your decision.

_____

_____

_____

_____

_____

_____

_____

_____

_____

See page 117 for the court's decision.

Case Study 2

Mr. Smith was not very popular among the secretaries, primarily because of his sexual advances, which—when rejected—created difficulty in the working relationship. Some of the secretaries got together and went to Mr. Smith's boss to complain. The company investigated the situation at once. When the women, worried that they might be fired, asked for a written assurance that they wouldn't be, they were not given one, although they were given verbal assurances. They were asked not to contact the Equal Employment Opportunity Commission during the course of the investigation.

Ultimately, Mr. Smith was put on leave, and then demoted. During the investigation, the women took their case to court, claiming liability against the company.

Would you have held the company liable for the actions of Mr. Smith? Explain.

_____

_____

_____

_____

_____

_____

_____

_____

_____

_____

_____

_____

_____

See page 117 for the court's decision.

Case Study 3

The president of a large company was aware of the tremendous sales being made by Joe Jones, a sales manager at a competitor's firm. The president sent several of his sales representatives to contact Mr. Jones in an attempt to lure him to their firm. They cited the benefits: Mr. Jones could have a larger budget, he would have a bigger staff, and he would be joining a firm that gave employees ample time to establish their worth. Mr. Jones agreed. He signed a one-year contract, the renewal of which would be determined by the company president, and then went to work.

Unfortunately, the company president retired shortly after Mr. Jones began. Mr. Jones's efforts were not as successful as everyone had hoped, and at the end of the year, the new president informed Mr. Jones that his contract would not be renewed.

Mr. Jones took the matter to court. How do you think the case was decided?

_____

_____

_____

_____

_____

_____

_____

_____

_____

_____

_____

_____

See page 118 for the court's decision.

Case Study 4

Mr. Johnson had 25 years experience in his field before being hired to be executive director of a security guard service. For the 7 years he has been there, he has turned the company around and performed all essential functions of his job and more. In the last year, Mr. Johnson was diagnosed with terminal brain cancer. Recently he was fired because the company claimed he could not do his job. Should the company rethink its decision?

See page 118 for the court's decision.

✍ Worksheet 10
Workers' Rights Legislation

Here is a quick test to see how knowledgeable you are about legislation protecting workers' rights. If you do not do well on the test and if you are responsible for frequent hiring, you should do some reading on legal issues or take courses that cover such issues.

1. A 39-year-old employee was fired and an 18-year-old was hired to replace him. Will the employee who was fired win an age discrimination lawsuit?
   Yes _____ No _____

2. In special circumstances, do employers have the right to discriminate based on sex, national origin, or religion?
   Yes _____ No _____

3. Can an employee be terminated without legal repercussions for the employer if that employee has filed a discrimination suit that is proven to have no validity?
   Yes _____ No _____

4. An individual's constitutional right to free speech means he or she cannot be fired for speaking out against an employer. Is this true?
   Yes _____ No _____

5. Can an employer require an employee to dress in a certain way?
   Yes _____ No _____

6. May an employer ask how many days an applicant was absent from work during the last year due to illness?
   Yes _____ No _____

See page 118 for legal interpretations.

Success Strategies From...

Stephen M. Karas, First Vice President, Manager of Major Buildings Division for Security Pacific Bank

On Firing: "When it becomes necessary to terminate someone, I also feel a responsibility. I ask myself, 'Did I do everything I could to assist this person? Did I communicate properly? Did he or she have all the necessary tools to do the job?'"

On Hiring: "As far as hiring is concerned, I look beyond qualifications. I use my people skills, my years of experience, to determine if this is the right person for the job we have available."

Success Strategies From...

Jane Stallman, Manager, Professional Development, Lockheed Advanced Development Company

On Hiring
and Firing:
"The cost of a poor selection is not only in dollars. It is also in disruption, morale, and emotional energy. Establishing position selection criteria as well as technical criteria is the first step toward a successful selection. Behavioral criteria as well as technical criteria are essential. Think through what you will really need because if you do not, you are likely to get out of the selection exactly what you put into it."

During the Termination Meeting

1

If termination seems like the only possible alternative, check with the appropriate personnel to ensure that you have followed all the necessary policies.

2

Be as considerate as you can. Firings are difficult but not fatal.

3

Make the meeting as brief as possible.

5

During the Termination Meeting

■ **If termination seems like the only possible alternative, check with the appropriate personnel—your supervisor, the union representatives, the personnel department, possibly even the corporate attorney—to ensure that you have followed all the necessary policies.**

According to Robert Half, 80 percent of us have been fired at one time or another. And most of the time, the firing was expected. When it becomes abundantly clear that firing an employee is the only possible recourse, you owe it to the employee to act decisively. Since the employee probably already knows the termination is imminent, chances are he or she will be relieved that the decision is finally made, providing the opportunity to find another job or another firm for which he or she is better suited. In time, the person you are firing will probably be grateful to you for having forced him or her take the first step on a new career path

Make certain you have followed corporate policies. Have the severance pay ready, if you can. If outplacement services are available, have the information regarding them available to give to the employee at this time. In short, do all you can to enable the person to leave quickly, quietly, and proudly.

■ **Be as considerate as you can. Firings are difficult but not fatal.**

The most uncomfortable part of the termination interview is probably the first few minutes. There will be tension and awkwardness since the employee has probably guessed why the meeting has been called. And you, too, will be feeling some anxiety, since being fired has a tremendous impact on a person's life. You might begin the meeting with a sentence such as this:

> "George, I suspect you know why I have called you in today. I would like us to deal with this issue of termination quickly and cleanly. I would also like to assure you that the company will continue to treat you fairly. Your severance check has been prepared, and we will have outplacement services available to you for the next week."

Ask whether the person would like to officially resign rather than be fired. Also ask what he or she would like colleagues to be told.

Give thought to the kind of work or industry in which the employee's talents would be better utilized and try to have a few leads available, if only the name of an employment agency that might be useful. You may also have heard of job openings in other companies that might be of interest to the employee. In other words, make the termination meeting as painless as possible.

Firing Rule of Thumb:

Treat the other person as you would like to be treated.

■ **Make the meeting as brief as possible.**

In the interest of all concerned, make the actual termination meeting as brief as possible. The employee has no doubt been expecting this meeting. If the employee is surprised by it, then you have failed to do an adequate job of helping the employee and keeping him or her apprised of your intentions.

Do not review old sources of dispute. Make the parting of the ways as cordial but as definitive as you can. This meeting can be likened to a divorce—not to a possible reconciliation. Keep it clean, crisp, and quick.

Also strive to reduce the amount of time the employee will have to remain "on the job." Ideally, you will have the severance check ready so that all the employee has to do is clear his or her desk, say good-bye to colleagues, and leave the office. If the employee remains on the job for the next several days, you can be fairly certain not much work will get done. In all likelihood, the employee will be engaged in destructive thinking and talking about you and the company.

Instead, the terminated individual should be engaged in more constructive actions, such as looking for a new job. Do not permit the fired employee to have a negative impact on the department's morale.

> **"People are rarely fired for incompetence. It's not getting along that's almost always the underlying reason for dismissal."**
>
> —*Stuart Margulies*

✍ Worksheet 11
Opening Statements
for the Termination Meeting

Use this exercise to prepare an opening statement for the termination
meeting and to note other information you must convey to the employee. Consider such options as continuing health care benefits, when
keys to the office must be turned in, when personal articles should be
removed from the office, and so forth.

_____

_____

_____

_____

_____

_____

_____

_____

_____

_____

_____

_____

_____

_____

_____

_____

_____

_____

_____

_____

Success Strategies From...

Jane Holcomb, Ph.D., Management Consultant, On-Target Training

On Firing: "My advice on firing is always the same: Document. Document. Document. If you have not been documenting all along, you will have a problem when it comes to firing."

On Hiring: "Hire someone with the right personality for the job. Job skills can be taught; personality skills cannot be. For example, if you hire a salesperson, you can teach him or her sales skills. But, you cannot transform a shy, retiring personality into an extroverted one. It is futile to try."

Tobie Wolf, Employee Development Specialist, United States Office of Personnel Management

On Hiring: "A selection panel can improve the hiring process by increasing the points of view on which selection decisions are based. Experienced peer-level employees are often able to ask and answer questions regarding details that are not apparent to higher management."

After the Termination Meeting

1

Conduct an exit interview.

2

Learn from the experience and make changes accordingly.

6

After the Termination Meeting

■ Conduct an exit interview.

Once the employee adjusts to the reality of the firing, he or she is in a better position to put things in perspective and to give an honest assessment of why his or her relationship with the company reached the termination point. Exit interviews should be conducted within three days of the termination meeting. If that meeting has been handled well, you should also conduct the exit interview. If for some reason, however, you are not on good terms with the employee, have a member of the personnel department conduct the interview and explore with the employee the events that led to the separation.

Here are some of the areas you may wish to address with your questions:

- How to better ensure that employee talents and company requirements match

- How to avoid termination procedures for similar reasons in the future

- How the employee feels about his or her former supervisor, department, job, and company

- What the employee would have done in the same situation had he or she been the supervisor

It is a good idea to tape record the answers or take notes as the terminated employee responds. You may even wish to give the questionnaire to the employee prior to the exit interview.

Ask whether you can call the employee in six months just to learn how he or she is doing. And then follow through on your request. Chances are, the person will be gainfully and happily employed by that time. Knowing this will confirm that you have done the right thing. It will also enable you to confidently tell others in a similar situation that termination is often the only way to achieve a win-win situation for everyone involved.

■ Learn from the experience and make changes accordingly.

Study the answers the employee gives during this final interview. You will, in all likelihood, learn some things from the exit interview, indeed from the whole termination process. Use the valuable information you have gathered to make appropriate changes in the hiring process, the performance appraisal process, the counseling process, perhaps even in your own behavior. Without taking offense, try to analyze the mistakes you may have made so you can avoid making them in the future. If the company erred in some way (for example, the hiring procedures may not have been thorough enough), take the initiative to bring about change in those procedures. There is no growth if there is no change. Supervisors can improve their performance only if they are constantly assessing it and modifying the way they usually operate.

In time, as you perfect your hiring abilities, you will have fewer and fewer opportunities to perfect your firing abilities. And this will be the best of all possible work-related worlds.

> **"**If a person can't do something, go back to goal setting. If a person won't do something, reprimand.**"**
>
> —*Kenneth H. Blanchard*
> *and Robert Lorber*

Success Strategies From...

Diane Hammar, Principal of Helendale Road School, Irondequoit, New York

"All firings are difficult. But firing a teacher is especially difficult because teachers are protected by tenure. There are only two official grounds for dismissal — morality and incompetence — and both are nearly impossible to substantiate. The best approach is to supervise nontenured teachers very closely; if there are any doubts about their capability, they should not be granted tenure.

"Education is unique in the protection it provides — a lifetime guarantee of employment, actually — to individuals who have passed the probationary period. A further problem, of course, is that teachers may be outstanding early in their careers, especially during the three-year probationary period, but may become complacent later on. In education, we are faced with all the usual firing sensitivities but a few additional ones as well."

Summary

Before the Termination Meeting

■ Maintain an open dialogue with the employee who may be having trouble. Begin the process informally.

■ Make the meetings and your recordkeeping more formal if the problem persists.

■ Protect yourself and your company against wrongful discharge lawsuits.

During the Termination Meeting

■ If termination seems like the only possible alternative, check with the appropriate personnel — your boss, the union, the Personnel Department, possibly even the corporate attorney — to ensure you have followed all necessary policies.

■ Be as considerate as you can. Firings are difficult but not fatal.

■ Make the meeting as brief as possible.

After the Termination Meeting

■ Conduct an exit interview.

■ Learn from the experience and make changes accordingly.

In Closing

This handbook has tried to make the hiring and firing processes as painless as possible by presenting the general principles to be followed in most hiring and firing situations. Be aware, however, that in some fields, such as education and government, special hiring and firing considerations apply. Federal employees, for example, usually must pass standard written examinations as a prerequisite to employment. And, in the field of education, tenure offers teachers a unique type of job protection.

Whether the hiring or firing circumstances are those traditionally found in corporate America or the special circumstances that apply to certain fields, the hiring and firing processes can be difficult for both parties. There is no guarantee that you will hire the perfect person every time you have an opening. Nor is there any certainty that you will never have to fire an employee whose work is less than satisfactory. But if you keep the long-range perspective in mind and treat other human beings with respect, you should be able to create situations in which both parties profit. Now that you have familiarized yourself with the general principles discussed in this book, you should be well on your way to achieving a win-win solution to any hiring or firing situation you encounter.

Appendices

A

Forms for the Hiring Process

Interview Checklist

Use this checklist to ensure that you adhere to your company's policies regarding interviews.

❑ 1. Are there special employment interview guidelines that the personnel department or upper management wishes to have followed? If so, list them here.

_____

_____

_____

_____

_____

❑ 2. What special documents do I want to show the applicant?

_____

_____

_____

_____

_____

❑ 3. What areas of the building should the applicant see? Are these areas accessible as defined in Title III of the Americans with Disabilities Act of 1990?

_____

_____

_____

_____

_____

❑ 4. Who else should the applicant meet? (Be certain to check in advance to be sure these people are available.)

_____

_____

_____

_____

_____

❑ 5.　Here is the information I will convey regarding:

salary _____

_____

_____

_____

performance reviews _____

_____

_____

_____

training _____

_____

_____

the likelihood of travel/relocation _____

_____

_____

_____

probationary period _____

_____

_____

_____

flex time/overtime/vacations _____

_____

_____

_____

the benefits package _____

_____

_____

_____

additional items _____

_____

_____

_____

■ Candidate Evaluation Form A

INTERVIEW FORM			
Job _____ Applicant _____ Date _____			

Criteria / Critical Skills	Job Task	Question	Comment
1.			
2.			
3.			
4.			
5.			
6.			
7.			
8.			

■ Candidate Evaluation Form B

INTERVIEW FORM					
Job _____ Applicant _____ Date _____					
Criteria / Critical Skills	**Importance**	**X**	**Applicant's Score**	**=**	**Skill Score**
1.					
2.					
3.					
4.					
5.					
6.					
7.					
8.					

Total Score for Candidate = _____

Comments: _____

_____

_____

■ Interviewer Self-Assessment Form

Use this form to evaluate yourself after each interview. Circle the
answers that apply or provide a brief explanation.

1. Did I put the applicant at ease?   Yes   No

2. Who did most of the talking?   Me   Applicant

3. What question evoked the most revealing answer from the
    candidate?

    _____

    _____

    _____

    _____

4. What question revealed the least valuable information?

    _____

    _____

    _____

    _____

5. Did I listen well?   Yes   No

6. Did I use silence well?   Yes   No

7. Did I close the interview well?   Yes   No

8. What should I do differently next time?

    _____

    _____

    _____

    _____

■ Telephone Reference Check Sheet

Use this sheet to record information you obtain about the candidate during telephone reference checks.

Applicant name _____

Position applied for _____

Name of reference _____

Company _____ Phone _____

1. Good morning. My name is Mary Smith. I am the Personnel Director at ABC Widget Company. I am making this reference call regarding Tim Allen, who has applied for the position of budget analyst here. He has given us your name as a reference. Could you tell me the dates of his employment at your company?
   From _____ to _____

2. What was his position at your company?
   _____

   What was his salary? _____

   What were his job duties? _____

3. What would you say was the applicant's most significant contribution to the company?
   _____
   _____

4. Would you rehire this person if you had a chance? Why or why not?
   _____
   _____

5. Could you identify any problems this employee had in the performance of his job?
   _____
   _____

6. Could you share any other information that might assist us in making our decision?
   _____
   _____

Thank you for your time.

Forms for the Firing Process

Discipline Form

Pretermination Questionnaire
for Supervisors

Exit Interview Questionnaire

■ Discipline Form

1. What do I hope to accomplish as a result of this discipline meeting?

    _____
    _____
    _____
    _____

2. What exactly would I like to have the employee do differently?

    _____
    _____
    _____
    _____

3. What specific observations will I bring to the employee's attention and what effect (positive, negative, neutral) will they have on the employee? (In other words, how is the employee likely to respond? What will the employee say?)

My observations	The likely effect on the employee
_____	_____
_____	_____
_____	_____
_____	_____
_____	_____
_____	_____

4. What will I say in response to the employee's reactions?

    _____
    _____
    _____
    _____

5. What is the agreement I hope we can reach?

    _____
    _____
    _____
    _____

■ Pretermination Questionnaire for Supervisors

Before making that final and most serious decision about letting an employee go, fill out this questionnaire. If you have difficulty completing it, it may be that you have been premature in your judgment and that the employee deserves another chance. On the other hand, if you can answer these questions easily, without bias, then you are probably operating with fairness and doing the best thing for all parties.

1. Prior to this recent period of difficulty, what has been the employee's work record?

    _____

    _____

2. Could this present difficulty be rooted in a personality conflict rather than the employee's inability to do the work?

    Yes ❑ No ❑   If so, how could that conflict be resolved?

    _____

    _____

3. Has the employee been treated fairly? Has the employee been given an adequate number of opportunities to improve? Do I have all the facts—have I listened to both sides? Would I feel I had been dismissed for good reason if the circumstances were reversed?

    _____

    _____

4. Have I given the employee the tools and training necessary to do the job that was expected?

    _____

    _____

5. Do my actions compare in severity to those taken in similar cases in the past?

    _____

    _____

6. What will be the consequences of dismissing this particular employee? Might I regret my decision?

    _____

    _____

■ Exit Interview Questions

1. In retrospect, what could have been done at what point to ensure that the fit between your talents and our requirements was the best possible?

   _____

   _____

   _____

   _____

   _____

   _____

2. What suggestions can you make to help us avoid having to undergo such termination procedures in the future?

   _____

   _____

   _____

   _____

   _____

   _____

3. How do you feel about your former supervisor, department, job, and this company as you prepare to leave? If you had been the supervisor in this situation, what would you have done?

   _____

   _____

   _____

   _____

   _____

4. Additional questions or comments:

   _____

   _____

   _____

   _____

   _____

   _____

Worksheet Answers

Worksheet 1: Past Hiring and Firing Experiences (p. 4)

Answers will vary.

Worksheet 2: Critical Employment Questions (p. 24)

Answers will vary.

Worksheet 3: Avoiding Interview Stereotypes (p. 33)

Answers will vary, but in general avoid stereotyping candidates according to:

- The way they are dressed.
- Their physical appearance (height, weight, hair color, overall looks, etc.).
- Their level of education, particularly candidates who appear overqualified.
- Their tendency to be either shy or talkative.
- A physical or mental impairment that they have had, that they have now, or that you perceive them to have.

Worksheet 4: Employment Interview Script (p. 37)

Compare the notes you made in the "Comments" section to the following critique of the employment interview at Jax Crackers Company. The numbers in the left margin correspond to the paragraph numbers of the Interview Script.

1   Mr. Jax should not have addressed the candidate as Susie.
He should have formally introduced himself.
He should not have discussed a previous applicant.
He should not have asked the previous applicant about her family.
Such a question constitutes an unfair inquiry.
Telling about a candidate who cried during the interview probably caused fear or discomfort for Susan Klem. It was not the sort of statement that would have relaxed her.

3   Mr. Jax made no effort to put the applicant at ease. For example, he did not ask whether she would like a cup of coffee.
Clearly, Mr. Jax' schedule was too tight. Twenty minutes is not enough time for an in-depth interview, especially if there will be more than one interviewer.
Mr. Jax was not organized or prepared for the interview.
Asking the candidate about her name was an unfair inquiry.

5   Asking Susan Klem about her marital status was also an unfair inquiry.

7   Asking about physical or mental disabilities is unlawful under the Americans with Disabilities Act of 1990.
Mr. Jax wastes interview time by detailing all of his problems.

He virtually assures the candidate she has the job—"That's why I need you."

9   He has no job description available.
     He turns control of the interview over to the candidate when he asks that she begin with her questions.

10   Mr. Jax should not be reading while the applicant is speaking.

11   Most women find it offensive to be referred to as a "girl."
     The reference to Susan Klem's appearance is inappropriate, and the wink could be construed as sexually offensive behavior.
     Interviewers cannot ask whether an applicant can work on a weekend. Such a question could be viewed as an inquiry about religious preferences.

12   As a courtesy, Mr. Jax should have informed the applicant that more than one person would be interviewing her. Ideally, both interviewers would be present from the very start of the interview. Further, Mr. Jax never introduces Mr. Pryze and Susan Klem.

13   Again, Mr. Jax speaks as if Susan Klem already has the job and is virtually guaranteeing her a promotion.

14   This question is considered an unfair inquiry because it allows the interviewer to learn the applicant's age and might, therefore, be a source of age discrimination.

16   Mr. Jax rushes the applicant through the interview in an almost rude manner.
     His scheduling was very poor.
     He asks three questions in a row.
     The question about hobbies is irrelevant, as is the question about the applicant's zodiac sign.
     The question about the organizations to which she might belong violates Title VII legislation.

18   The inquiry about the candidate's church is an unfair inquiry.
     Mr. Jax should have made arrangements not to be interrupted by phone calls while the interview was being conducted.

Worksheet 5: Developing Open-Ended Questions (p. 44)

These answers may differ from yours. The idea is to ask candidates questions that will provoke a complete response rather than a one-word response.

1. Furnished

2. What are some situations that required you to work under pressure and how did you handle them?

3. What is your approach to solving problems?

4. Describe a situation in which you had a task to learn quickly and explain how you handled it.

5. Describe your experience as a purchasing agent. What companies have you worked for in this capacity?

6. In what ways do you express your creativity on the job?

7. Tell me about some of the projects or processes you have been involved with that were improved as a result of your contributions.

8. How do you handle responsibility?

9. Tell me how you go about organizing tasks and responsibilities.

10. What things in particular are satisfying about the work you do?

Worksheet 6: Identifying Question Types (p. 46)

1. L

2. E

3. Y/N

4. C

5. E

6. Y/N and E

7. C

8. Y/N

9. L

10. E

Worksheet 7: Identifying Training Methods (p. 68)

Answers may vary. Here are some ideas for training employees when you don't have a budget to do so.

1. Have lunchtime lectures with presentations by local experts or college professors.

2. Start a library of related materials and circulate pertinent information.

3. Publish a column each month regarding training issues. Use the company newspaper or create a special newsletter.

4. Produce a video showing employees at work using their skills.

5. Encourage employees to train one another.

6. Start each staff meeting with a brief presentation by an employee who has learned a new skill.

Worksheet 8: Developing Opening Dialogues With Problem Employees (p. 69)

Answers will vary. Keep in mind that you cannot directly ask employees about their personal lives.

Worksheet 9: Avoiding Wrongful Discharge Suits (p. 79)

Case Study 1

The lower court that initially tried the case sided with the company. However, upon appeal, the state supreme court ruled for the plaintiff, stating that no one should be threatened or reprimanded for refusing to break the law.

When companies have established procedures, such as hotlines, which enable employees to report instances of alleged wrongdoing, problems can be rectified long before they reach the litigation stage. Ethical practices should be insisted upon; violations should not be swept under the rug. And the "whistleblowers" who bring illegal situations into the open should be praised, not punished.

Case Study 2

The court found the company liable, despite its efforts to reprimand Mr. Smith. The firm was wrong, the court ruled, to leave Mr. Smith as the boss of the two women who had lodged the complaint against him. The company was also wrong to ask the women not to go to the EEOC while the investigation was going on. Finally, the court ruled that the company should have provided the written documentation the women had requested. The company was not quick enough to remove the source of harassment.

Case Study 3

The court felt that this case involved a breach of contract — Joe Jones had been told he would have ample time to establish his worth — and so ruled in favor of Mr. Jones, stating that the firm had not operated in good faith and had not been fair in its treatment of Mr. Jones.

Case Study 4

Title I of the Americans with Disabilities Act of 1990 prohibits employers from discriminating against a qualified individual with a disability who is able to perform the essential functions of the job with or without reasonable accommodation. Mr. Johnson has performed, and is continuing to perform, the essential functions of the job. Thus, the company is in error for firing Mr. Johnson.

Worksheet 10:   Workers' Rights Legislation (p. 83)

1. The Age Discrimination in Employment Act of 1967 (ADEA) protects employees over the age of 40. So, a 39-year-old would not win a lawsuit since the federal act has not been violated. (In Oregon, the statute against age discrimination applies to anyone 18 years of age or older.)

2. Title VII is the section of the Civil Rights Act of 1964 that deals with discrimination. Title VII *does* allow discrimination if sex, religion, or national origin is a "bona fide occupational qualification" that can be considered a business necessity. For example, religion could be an important qualification for a military chaplain.

3. Companies must base their decision on the basis of an employee's work-related conduct, performance, and suitability, not on the basis of suits filed against them.

4. There have been numerous cases in which the right of free speech was balanced against the efficient operation of an office. Judges have refused

to reinstate discharged employees whose comments caused disharmony among workers. Other cases supporting the dismissal have been based on statements that violated confidentiality or statements that were libelous.

5. An employer cannot require an employee to dress a certain way if the dress can be viewed as sexual harassment. For example, if a woman is asked to wear a revealing costume, she can refuse and not suffer any consequences as a result.

6. It is unlawful to inquire whether an applicant has a disability or to ask questions that would screen out a person with medical problems or a disability.

Worksheet 11: Opening Statements for the Termination Meeting (p. 90)

Answers will vary.

Available From
SkillPath Publications

Self-Study Sourcebooks

Climbing the Corporate Ladder: What You Need to Know and Do to Be a Promotable Person *by Barbara Pachter and Marjorie Brody*

Discovering Your Purpose *by Ivy Haley*

Mastering the Art of Communication: Your Keys to Developing a More Effective Personal Style *by Michelle Fairfield Poley*

Organized for Success! 95 Tips for Taking Control of Your Time, Your Space, and Your Life *by Nanci McGraw*

Productivity Power: 250 Great Ideas for Being More Productive *by Jim Temme*

Promoting Yourself: 50 Ways to Increase Your Prestige, Power, and Paycheck *by Marlene Caroselli, Ed.D.*

Risk-Taking: 50 Ways to Turn Risks Into Rewards *by Marlene Caroselli, Ed.D. and David Harris*

The Technical Writer's Guide *by Robert McGraw*

Total Quality Customer Service: How to Make It Your Way of Life *by Jim Temme*

Write It Right! A Guide for Clear and Correct Writing *by Richard Andersen and Helene Hinis*

Spiral Handbooks

The ABC's of Empowered Teams: Building Blocks for Success *by Mark Towers*

Assert Yourself! Developing Power-Packed Communication Skills to Make Your Points Clearly, Confidently, and Persuasively *by Lisa Contini*

Breaking the Ice: How to Improve Your On-the-Spot Communication Skills *by Deborah Shouse*

121

The Care and Keeping of Customers: A Treasury of Facts, Tips and Proven Techniques for Keeping Your Customers Coming BACK! *by Roy Lantz*

Dynamic Delegation: A Manager's Guide for Active Empowerment *by Mark Towers*

Every Woman's Guide to Career Success *by Denise M. Dudley*

Hiring and Firing: What Every Manager Needs to Know *by Marlene Caroselli, Ed.D. with Laura Wyeth, Ms.Ed.*

How to Deal With Difficult People *by Paul Friedman*

Learning to Laugh at Work: The Power of Humor in the Workplace *by Robert McGraw*

Making Your Mark: How to Develop a Personal Marketing Plan for Becoming More Visible and More Appreciated at Work *by Deborah Shouse*

Meetings That Work *by Marlene Caroselli, Ed.D.*

The Mentoring Advantage: How to Help Your Career Soar to New Heights *by Pam Grout*

Minding Your Business Manners: Etiquette Tips for Presenting Yourself Professionally in Every Business Situation *by Marjorie Brody and Barbara Pachter*

Misspeller's Guide *by Joel and Ruth Schroeder*

NameTags Plus: Games You Can Play When People Don't Know What to Say *by Deborah Shouse*

Networking: How to Creatively Tap Your People Resources *by Colleen Clarke*

New & Improved! 25 Ways to Be More Creative and More Effective *by Pam Grout*

Power Write! A Practical Guide to Words That Work *by Helene Hinis*

Putting Anger to Work For You! *by Ruth and Joel Schroeder*

Reinventing Your Self: 28 Strategies for Coping With Change *by Mark Towers*

The Supervisor's Guide: The Everyday Guide to Coordinating People and Tasks *by Jerry Brown and Denise Dudley, Ph.D.*

Taking Charge: A Personal Guide to Managing Projects and Priorities *by Michal E. Feder*

Treasure Hunt: 10 Stepping Stones to a New and More Confident You! *by Pam Grout*

A Winning Attitude: How to Develop Your Most Important Asset! *by Michelle Fairfield Poley*

For more information, call 1-800-873-7545.